I LOVE BIRDS!

I LOVE BIRDS!

52 Ways to Wonder, Wander & Explore Birds with Kids

JENNiFER WARD

Illustrations by **ALEXANDER ViDAL**

ROOST BOOKS
2019

Roost Books
An imprint of Shambhala Publications, Inc.
4720 Walnut Street
Boulder, Colorado 80301
roostbooks.com

© 2019 by Jennifer Ward
Illustrations © 2019 by Alexander Vidal

9 8 7 6 5 4 3 2 1

First Edition
Printed in the United States of America

⊗This edition is printed on acid-free paper that meets the American National Standards Institute Z39.48 Standard.
♻Shambhala Publications makes every effort to print on recycled paper. For more information please visit www.shambhala.com.

Roost Books is distributed worldwide by Penguin Random House, Inc., and its subsidiaries.

Designed by Daniel Urban-Brown

Library of Congress Cataloging-in-Publication Data
Names: Ward, Jennifer, 1963– author. | Vidal, Alexander, illustrator.
Title: I love birds!: 52 ways to wonder, wander, and explore birds with kids
  / Jennifer Ward; illustrations by Alexander Vidal.
Description: Boulder, Colorado: Roost Books, 2019. | Audience: Ages 4 to 8.
  | Includes bibliographical references.
Identifiers: LCCN 2018011422 | ISBN 9781611804157 (paperback: alk. paper)
Subjects: LCSH: Bird watching. | Family recreation. | Outdoor recreation.
Classification: LCC QL677.5 .W335 2019 | DDC 598.072/34—dc23
LC record available at https://lccn.loc.gov/2018011422

CONTENTS

· · · · · · · · · · · · · · · · ·

FALL

WINTER

INTRODUCTION

. . . .

AS A YOUNG CHILD I recall lying in bed, tucked in silence and stillness. The light was dim and dusky, filling every nook and cranny in my room; I can still see this so vividly. Then, out of nowhere, one single birdcall pierced the quiet, separating night from morning. This call was joined by another call. And then more calls, the sounds building in crescendo, overlapping, high, low, melodic, and nonstop. The very air brimmed with song that is the *dawn chorus*. It was the first time I had ever experienced it, and even as a child I knew it was something magnificent. Experiencing it made me feel wondrous. It made me feel alive, special, and, most importantly, connected to the big, wide, wonderful world around me. To this day I continue to listen for it.

In 2008, my book *I Love Dirt!* was published. At that time, it was a call to parents, grandparents, educators, and caregivers to help recover one of the greatest joys in childhood: spending time outdoors in nature. We were in the midst of a true "nature deficit," a term coined by author and journalist Richard Louv. Children and adults alike living with overly busy schedules, engaged with screen time from sunup to sundown, seeking places where they could stay plugged in near electrical outlets, schools eliminating recess, and the like. Thanks to Richard Louv and many others, today a glorious movement is taking place—a wise awareness that spending time in nature is beneficial to our health and well-being. Research also supports the detrimental effects of living without nature.

It is a joyful thing to watch our children discover the world around them, and birds certainly enhance this experience. As a matter of fact, engaging with a simple bird feeder is one of the most common ways people may interact with wild animals. Birds can be found everywhere, high, low, wherever we go. As children discover the wonder, beauty, science, and souls of birds, we are given a priceless gift—experiencing the world through their eyes.

This book was born from one of my dearest passions: birds. Like *I Love Dirt!*, it offers fifty-two open-ended activities that will give the outdoors back to your children. In just five minutes, you can turn your child's world around, open their senses, and connect them to nature. *I Love Birds!* encourages your child to think, wonder, wander, explore, create, nurture, and have an amazing time with the avian wildlife that coexist with us day to day, month by month, and season by season.

Anywhere a bird might be spotted provides an opportunity for discovery. They bring the gift of nature to us wherever we may be. Be it a city sidewalk, an urban park, through a window, from a wheelchair, in a backyard, or even while lying in bed waiting for the dawn chorus—birds are waiting to be enjoyed and discovered! Time in nature is free of cost—as are the activities in this book—but the rewards that come with exploring birds will stay with your children for the rest of their lives, benefiting them and the planet they share with birds. Now get out there and soar!

Thank you for sharing *I Love Birds!* with the wee chicks

in your life. In this book you'll find a host of creative and engaging ways to better understand these winged wonders. The activities are categorized by the habits most birders practice:

- Observe: To know birds, you must observe birds. These activities offer ways to see, hear, and better understand birds and bird behavior.
- Take Note: Use this book (or get a trusty notebook) and write down the things you notice about birds and draw the birds you observe.
- Take Action: Become a better bird advocate by doing simple projects that support the birds in your area.

Ready to fly? Let's do this!

SPRING

1

· · ·

LOOK UP, LOOK DOWN, LOOK ALL AROUND

BIRDS ARE EVERYWHERE. They can be found flying through the sky, foraging high in treetops, filling the air with calls and songs, perching on power lines, scavenging on the ground, scaling tree trunks, racing surf on a shoreline, or bobbing on the surface of water, just to name a few places.

Connecting with birds is as simple as stepping outside and opening our eyes and ears to their presence. As we do so, we're connecting with wild animals right outside our back door! Yet, how often do we really observe birds and take note of them? Today, with technology at our fingertips 24-7, it's so easy for us to willingly ignore our surroundings. Set an intention to connect to the nature that surrounds you and your child, and let birds be your guide as you do.

OBSERVE

Find a spot outdoors where you and your child can relax. It can be a patch of grass, a sidewalk, a balcony, or a deck—anywhere, as long as you're comfortable and outside. Feel the air on your skin and face. Feel your feet on the ground below you. Observe all of the details around you: the color of the sky, the temperature, and even small weeds sprouting up in unusual places. Enjoy the stillness of nature and the calm it brings.

First, just listen. Absorb all the sounds around you. There may be traffic sounds, mechanical sounds, and wind-in-the-trees sounds. Through it all, listen for bird sounds: tweets, calls, chirps. Flapping wings, rap-rap-raps, and tap-tap-taps. Songs and coos. Seek out the bird sounds you hear and attempt to locate where the sounds are coming from. Often, we may hear a bird but never see it (or imagine we've seen it). Spotting them can sometimes be tricky!

Seek out birds that you can see. How many birds can you spot with your eyes? We may not always need to look up to find a bird. They may be at eye level or on the ground. Binoculars aren't necessary to observe birds. Of course, with practice, binoculars work well for bird watching, but there's much bird-life to see with the naked eye, such as a bird's shape, size, color, location, and behavior. As you listen for birds, ask these questions:

- How many different sounds, songs, or calls can you hear?
- How many birds can you find up high?
- How many birds can you find on the ground, down low?
- Can you hear a birdcall or song? How many different calls or songs?
- Can you find a large bird?
- Can you find a small bird?
- Can you find a colorful bird?
- Can you find a bird that's eating?
- Can you find a bird that's running or hopping on the ground?
- Can you find a bird that's flying?

Enjoy connecting to nature and the birds that call it home,

where you will experience calm and a sense of wonder in everything avian.

Promotes relaxation, attentiveness, and observation skills

HELP ME UNDERSTAND

Q: How many birds are there on the planet?
A: Species vary by region, but overall there are approximately 10,400 species of birds on the planet.

2

. . .

BILLIONS OF BIRDS

COME SPRING, billions of birds wing their way, often thousands of miles, from their southern winter grounds to their northern breeding grounds. As a result, April and May are very busy sky traffic periods on our planet. Nothing marks spring like the return of migratory birds!

You may awaken one morning to find high treetops and low shrubs bustling with birdsong and bird movement, birds busy hopping from limb to limb, activity that wasn't noticeable the day prior. This is because migratory songbirds traveled all night, and now they've stopped to rest and refuel. Some species will rest in your area for a few days and then continue their journey northward. Other species will arrive in your area and stay put for nesting and breeding through the summer. The strongest males arrive first, scouting out the best breeding areas. Once the females arrive, they choose the males with the ideal habitats for raising young.

Make a specific effort with your child to spend time outdoors in April and May to experience spring's bird migration, especially when weather conditions shift winds from south to north, as migratory birds take advantage of tailwinds. Then, simply look to the leaves! In addition to your *resident* birds—birds that remain in your area all year long—observe very carefully. Can you spy a species you've not noticed before? Search high in the treetops, among leaves and new growth, where colorful warblers may be hunting for spiders and insects. Look among shrubs and hedges and on the ground below them. Notice bird sounds: Is there a song or call that is unfamiliar or new? If so, chances are it is a migrant, weary and hungry. Perhaps it is just passing through and stopping to rest, and will continue northward. Or, perhaps it is a species that will summer and nest in your area with you.

TAKE NOTE

With your child, document the dates and details of migrants and first arrivals in your area during spring's migration. Using the details of your notes, reference a field guide to birds in your area to help identify species and become familiar with your region's species.

MY FOTS (FIRST OF THE SEASON)

Date:

Location:

Size:

Descriptive notes:

Sketch:

 Promotes awareness, understanding of the natural world, and observation skills

A FEAST FOR
FIRST ARRIVALS

APPROXIMATELY 40 PERCENT of our world's bird species migrate each spring and fall. As spring arrives, so do these weary travelers back to northern regions—and they arrive exhausted and hungry, many having flown hundreds or thousands of miles, often nonstop, using up the reserves of stored body fat. Migration is an extremely challenging and dangerous time for birds. They encounter harsh weather and a lack of adequate habitat to rest and refuel along their journey, among a host of other challenging elements.

As migrants arrive or stop to rest, most will be seeking protein in the source of bugs, but migration season is the perfect time to offer some additional food as well. Many migratory species, such as orioles and tanagers, will appreciate apple slices, grape jelly, and orange halves.

TAKE ACTION

Explain to your child that many birds are passing through your area, having traveled very long distances, and that they are extremely tired and hungry. Use a map to show the distance traveled by migrating species in your area, such as orioles. The Cornell Lab of Ornithology website or any bird field guide for your region will show the ranges of bird species by season, indicating where certain species breed during summer months and where they winter, and their migration routes in between.

Then, create a fresh offering of fruits and sustenance for these traveling birds, which they will greatly appreciate. You and your child will also be rewarded as you observe ravenous species stopping by to enjoy your offering.

First, simply slice an orange in half. Then, poke a small hole on the outside half of each orange, through the skin. Finally, place each orange section on the upward-facing tip of a shepherd's hook where your feeder(s) hang or on the tip of a tree's branch, or rest it on top of a firm bush or shrub. Birds will love this fresh fruit treat! Change the oranges every few days, keeping the citrus offering fresh. (A variation on this sweet treat is to scoop out most of the orange fruit, mix this fruit with grape jelly, and place the mixture back into the halved orange.)

Sliced and diced apples or fresh apple cores with seeds are also delicious treats that spring birds will enjoy. Simply place pieces on a tray where birds may land to access them. Change the apple pieces every few days to keep the offerings fresh.

Promotes stewardship and empathy

Q: How far do migrating birds travel?

A: It varies by species, but here are some interesting migration findings: the Arctic Tern holds the record for longest migration distance, approximately 25,000 miles, pole to pole (almost 50,000 miles roundtrip each year); the Bar-Tailed Godwit flies almost 7,000 miles without stopping (it holds the record for longest nonstop flight); the Blackpoll Warbler flies 2,300 miles nonstop for eighty-six hours; the tiny Ruby-Throated Hummingbird migrates a distance of 5,000 round-trip miles each year, and the Rufous Hummingbird makes the longest migratory journey of any bird in the world, per its body size compared to distance covered, traveling almost 8,000 miles round-trip each year from Alaska to Mexico.

THE DAWN CHORUS

GÖKOTTA is a Swedish word that translates to *waking up at dawn to hear the first birdsong of the day.* In America, we call this musical avian phenomenon *the dawn chorus.* Spring and summer are perfect times to experience this magical, remarkable sound, as this is the time that birds wake up and establish their territories and sing to attract mates.

Check to determine when sunrise will take place. Then, set your alarm so you and your child wake up at least fifteen minutes prior to sunrise. Once you awaken, make a cup of tea, hot cocoa, or coffee, and grab a blanket to snuggle up with your child if the air outside is chilly. Together, sit outside in the dark. Be mindful as you sit: Feel the air on your face. Listen to how loud the stillness and quiet-dark of a new day may sound. Enjoy the calmness and serenity of the planet, of everything around you. There's nowhere to rush to, just you and your child, sitting in the moment. Listening. Waiting, in the silent, sleepy world.

Soon, the call of just one bird will pierce the air and stillness.

First one call. Followed by another. And then another and another. Behold as sounds and calls coming from each and every direction fill the air. As the day lightens and the world awakens, the chorus will fade. Throughout the day, you and your child may make note of daily birdcalls, sounds, and songs. They will be present but nothing like that of the dawn chorus.

* *

Promotes wonder, relaxation, and awareness

HELP ME UNDERSTAND

Q: Why do birds sound so loud in the morning?

A: Cooler temperatures and still air in the early morning allow bird calls to travel and be heard more effectively.

5

· · ·

HOME TWEET HOME

NESTS ARE ASTOUNDING architectural and engineering feats—homes for birds that defy elements of weather while supporting and protecting very fragile eggs, and often at elevated heights. What's even more astonishing is the fact that these structures are deftly engineered and created by animals (birds) that lack fingers and opposable thumbs.

Come spring, the avian world is all about nesting as birds prepare to incubate eggs and raise chicks—the sole purpose of nesting. Birds get busy gathering materials for their homes: animal fur (and even dog hair!), twigs, natural fibers, grasses, dried leaves, moss, lichen, and most anything that is soft and stringy.

Unfortunately, birds also gather nesting materials that prove harmful to them, such as fishing line and other litter, which they may become tangled in. A combination of human litter and loss of habitat for birds causes this problem and also poses the largest threat to wild bird species, as nesting grounds, food sources, and natural habitats that support nesting are increasingly being developed and/or polluted by humans.

TAKE ACTION

Creating a nest helper ball is a wonderful way to offer birds safe and earth-friendly materials to utilize, while also providing you and your child a rich opportunity to observe bird-nesting behavior.

Explain to your child that just as he has a special bed to snuggle into at night and a cozy home to live in, birds raising families require a home, too. These homes are called nests, and they come in many shapes and sizes. Nests will be a safe and secure place for a mother bird to lay her eggs, where she, and often her mate—depending on the species—will incubate the eggs and care for the chicks until they *fledge*, or leave the nest. Providing materials for nesting birds will help them with their nest building. This nest helper ball is a great way to do it.

Easily bendable floral wire (the thicker the better)
Wire cutters
Nesting materials

- A variety of fibers such as jute (4 inches or less in length, as birds can get tangled in longer lengths)
- Cotton string
- Scraps of yarn, in neutral colors (to keep the nest hidden from predators)
- Bits of cotton
- Dried grasses
- Natural raffia
- Dried leaves

1. Cut off an 8- to 12-inch section of floral wire.
2. Bend the floral wire around and around, to create a hollow orb approximately 3 or 4 inches in diameter.
3. Gently stuff the center of the wire ball with a variety of nesting materials.
4. Attach a string to the ball, for hanging.

5. Hang your nest helper ball to a tree branch or anywhere a bird may access it. Watch and enjoy as birds help themselves, plucking and grabbing and dashing off with their nesting material. As materials are depleted, refill the ball.

✔ *Promotes creativity, stewardship, and conservation*

HELP ME UNDERSTAND

Q: Are all bird nests alike?

A: Birds make the most variety of homes, or nests, than any other wild animal in the world. Just a few types of bird nests include:

- Woven nests (male weaver birds create an intricate, woven nest)
- Sack nests (orioles weave a sack nest far out on a limb, high off the ground)
- Cup-shaped nests (hummingbirds make the smallest cup nest, using grasses, lichen, and spider's web)
- Cavity nests (woodpeckers carve a cavity nest inside a tree's trunk)
- Floating nests (grebes make a floating nest on water, anchoring it to rooted water plants)
- Ground nests (Killdeer nest directly on the ground)
- Stick nests (doves and eagles create nests using sticks)
- Mound nests (flamingos create a nest on the ground out of mud)

FEATHERY FIELD TRIP

JUST WHO'S IN your neighborhood anyway? Aren't you curious? Certain birds remain in your area year-round, as residents. Others are seasonal, spending a window of time in your area for wintering or breeding. Others pass through, stopping by briefly during their migration. It's remarkable to realize that each and every day holds a chance for a new discovery where birds are concerned, right in your own backyard and neighborhood!

Wonder about the birds in your area with your child, and make it an adventure to discover them together. As you begin to see and hear the birds in your neighborhood, you may find that the species in one area, such as in your backyard, are different than the species that inhabit your front yard or your neighbor's house or the house a block away.

Take a walk with your child, with the sole purpose of listening and watching for birds in your yard and around your neighborhood. Make it a field trip!

TAKE NOTE

Bring along a notebook and pen. Then, ask the following questions:

- Do you see the same species of birds in the front yard and the backyard?

- Do you see the same species of birds down the street?
- Do morning species differ from evening species?

With your child, create a list of all the birds you have seen in your backyard and neighborhood. Include the following details:

Date:

Time:

Species (my best guess):

Behavior (feeding, hopping, perching, singing, etc.):

Location (high/low, ground, sky, tree, etc.):

Sound or calls heard:

Promotes curiosity, observation, and awareness of surroundings and wildlife

HELP ME UNDERSTAND

Q: I see a lot of birds during the day, but where do these birds go at night?

A: Birds that are active during the day, *diurnal* birds, sleep during the night. Some sleep in tree cavities or nooks and crevices, which shelter them from weather. Others sleep in birdhouses or in dense shrubs. Some sleep perched in trees. And some gather to sleep, or *roost*, in large flocks, such as blackbirds. Birds tuck their bills into their shoulders or backs, where the air is warmed by their body temperature. They fluff and puff their feathers to keep their bodies insulated when temperatures are cold, too.

7

...

SPLASHY TWEET RETREAT

WATER SOURCES are important to all living things, and birds are no exception. Birds require water year-round for survival. They will both drink and bathe in the water source you provide. Birds are attracted to drips, ponds, puddles, plants and rocks that "pool," and sprays and mists—really any water source will be a welcome delight for them!

You can attract birds and assist in their well-being by creating and offering a simple birdbath. Once you do, it will offer great joy for you and your child as you observe birds while they drink and bathe. Sometimes birds may even wait in line for a turn at the water you provide, or you may notice several birds or several different species drinking simultaneously.

There is nothing is more joyful than watching a bird take a bath, either, as they immerse their heads and bodies under water, rolling, fluffing, and shaking water everywhere. It is bird bliss!

TAKE ACTION

Explain to your child how fortunate we are to have water sources in our homes: faucets for drinking water and bathing. But what about wildlife? What about the birds in our yard? They need to drink water and take baths, too, just like we do. Take action and offer a water source for your bird neighbors. Then, feel good knowing you're helping to sustain a habitat necessary for wild birds and their health and survival. It will be fun to experience birds at your water source, too. Here are some tips for creating a splashy tweet retreat:

- You don't need to buy a birdbath. Any shallow pan will work as a water source for birds. It should not be very deep, 2 to 3 inches is plenty. Stone, ceramic, or plastic trays, such as those used for flowerpots, are an ideal depth. A ceramic dog bowl will work well, too.
- Water must always be fresh. Dump, wipe, and refill with fresh water at least every other day.
- Birds enjoy visiting water sources that are on a pedestal or on the ground. Create your splashy retreat near a shrub or potted plant so birds have a safe place to retreat for drying off. If possible, place it near a window where you may observe birds while you're inside as they bathe and drink outside.
- Place a large rock or several pebbles in the center of your birdbath, protruding out from the water's surface. Or, place a small tree branch across the birdbath's surface. The birds will perch upon the branch or rocks. This also helps birds judge the depth of the water.

Promotes stewardship, curiosity, and an appreciation for avian wildlife

As you begin observing birds at your birdbath, you'll notice they don't all drink the same way. Some species dip their beaks in and sip, while others dip their beaks in the water, then raise up their beaks to swallow the water they've captured. How many different drinking behaviors can you spy?

HELP ME UNDERSTAND

Q: Do all birds take baths?

A: Feathers are one characteristic unique to birds, and bathing is a very important part of feather maintenance for them. But birds don't bathe in just water. Birds may also bathe in the sun, stretching out their wings and allowing the ultraviolet rays to disinfect their feathers. You may also notice birds bathing in dust and sand, moving and rolling around as if in water. Dirt baths also help maintain a healthy plumage, cleaning feathers and helping to balance oil levels.

8

...

A RUSTIC ROOST

YOU'LL OFTEN SEE colorful and embellished bird-houses available for purchase, but think about it: with the exception of bowerbirds, how often do we see colorful bird-made nests in the wild? Do birds want colorful houses? There's a reason female birds are often more drab in color than their male counterparts: to camouflage them. Being camouflaged helps to protect female birds from predators while sitting patiently and stationary upon the nest during egg incubation and chick rearing. The last thing a mother bird needs while incubating eggs and caring for her chicks is unwanted attention.

In the wild, bird nests are also often camouflaged so that they blend in with their natural surroundings. They're designed with natural elements and meld seamlessly with the trees, shrubs, or landscapes where they were created. A bird nest is a vulnerable space: danger prowls at every turn in the form of predators, such as hungry snakes, mammals, and even other birds.

Supplying a birdhouse for nesting birds is an engaging and fun way to observe birds in the wild as a family unit. It provides an opportunity to watch a mother and father bird come and go as they fill it with found and gathered nesting materials, search for food, and feed their young. And if you're lucky, you may even experience the miraculous journey as the chicks fledge from their nest. In addition to these intrinsic joys, it also offers a habitat for birds during nesting season.

TAKE ACTION

Design a rustic, natural birdhouse with your child—one that is simple, subtle, functional, and beautiful. Create a house that will harmonize with nature while also providing shelter for the next generation of a wild bird family.

1 standard, simple wooden birdhouse from your local bird or
   garden store
Natural materials for decorating
- Twigs
- Bark
- Pine cones
- Driftwood
- Leaves
- Small branches
- Moss
- Small pebbles
Glue gun and glue sticks

Embellish your standard birdhouse with natural materials, using a glue gun or glue sticks to attach as few or as many items as you'd like. There's no right or wrong way to design a rustic birdhouse. The idea is simple, and the design is 100 percent yours and your child's.

Once finished, hang your rustic roost outdoors from a porch eave or on a pole with a predator baffle, which will protect it from predators such as hungry raccoons or snakes. Your birdhouse will not only blend beautifully with the environment, but it will also provide shelter and comfort to a feathered family. At the end of each nesting season (fall and winter), dispose of any nesting materials from inside the birdhouse to help keep it clean and ready for spring nesting once again.

· ·

 Promotes creativity, empathy, and stewardship

HELP ME UNDERSTAND

Q: What should I do if I find a baby bird on the ground?

A: If you find a baby bird with feathers on the ground and he appears helpless, he has likely fledged (left the nest) and is trying to figure out how to use his wings and feet to fly and land, not unlike a toddler taking his first steps. This "first time out of nest" process may take a day or two, and 99.9 percent of the time, his mom and dad are nearby, keeping an eye on the situation and feeding him. Resist the urge to intervene. If you find a naked nestling on the ground, it may have fallen from its nest due to a storm or a predator may have pulled it out. Look around for its nest, and if located, place it back in the nest. If you can't locate a nest, contact a bird rehabber in your area.

DID YOU KNOW?

Bird babies fall into two categories: *precocial* and *altricial*. Precocial birds open their eyes soon after hatching and quickly leave the nest, following the mother around for food (think chickens, ducks, and shorebirds). Altricial chicks have two stages of development: *nestling* and *fledgling*. They are born blind, featherless, and helpless and remain in their nest where parents keep them warm, fed, and sheltered until they are ready to *fledge*, or leave the nest. Bird parents must also constantly forage for food to feed their chicks. Nest time is a very busy time for bird parents!

BIRDS IN MOTION

SPRING IS SUCH a welcome season, with fresh, green growth and longer days following winter's chilly and gray days where it's often a challenge to play outdoors. Come spring, sunshine and warmer temperatures beckon. It's the perfect time to get outside and stretch your wings, at long last.

Take your wee chick under your wing and get outdoors.

While you're out there, make it a challenge to spy on birds, observing the many ways they move and enjoy spring weather. Birds are just as excited about springtime as humans: there are bugs to be caught for breakfast, lunch, and dinner—and snacks in between, finally! There are mates to attract and nest materials to gather. Birds are getting busy! You'll also see that they move in many different ways.

OBSERVE

How many different ways do birds move? Can you find these behaviors?

- A bird flapping its wings
- A bird soaring
- A bird hopping
- A bird walking
- A bird pecking
- A bird waddling
- A bird perching
- A bird singing or calling
- A bird running
- A bird gathering nesting materials
- A bird pulling on a worm

Turn your observations into a game of Simon Says. Use bird behaviors as commands:

SIMON SAYS . . .

"Hop" like a sparrow

"Flap your wings" like a wren

"Soar" like a hawk

"Waddle" like a duck

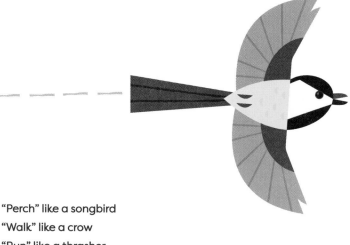

"Perch" like a songbird
"Walk" like a crow
"Run" like a thrasher
"Gather" like a robin
"Strut" like a pigeon

The playtime will be invigorating. You may even enjoy this game indoors during inclement weather.

✓ *Encourages observation skills, verbal skills, exercise, and well-being*

HELP ME UNDERSTAND

Q: Do all birds fly?
A: Not all birds can fly. For example, emus, kiwis, ostriches, and penguins are birds that do not fly. There are approximately forty species of birds that do not fly, but none of them live in North America.

10

......

DRAW THAT BIRD!

USING A FIELD GUIDE with your child for bird identification purposes is a wonderful method to properly ID birds you encounter. However, sometimes it's
tricky to identify a bird out in the wild. After all, the bird will
not sit and patiently wait while you flip through your guide
book. Birds are busy. They have places to go and things to do.

An alternative method to help you and your child easily
identify birds you encounter is to practice sketching them
as you watch them in their environment. With your sketch
and notes in hand, you may later, at your leisure, reference
a field guide to compare your field sketches and notes to
various species, ultimately and hopefully identifying the
birds you noted. It's a fun challenge to learn bird names
and to properly ID them. An important element is to not
take the process too seriously. Have fun with it, keeping
in mind that even bird experts wind up scratching their
heads in wonder with bird ID at times, too!

TAKE NOTE

You don't need to be an artist to sketch the birds you see!
Practice and have fun. Keep your drawings loose and simple as you follow these steps:

1. Create a roundish head.

2. Create an oval body.

3. Sketch the general length and angle of the tail.

4. Sketch the general shape and size of the beak.

Once you've sketched your bird, make notes to describe specific details you observed: the bird's behavior (was it hopping, running, flying, calling, feeding/foraging?), its location, sounds you heard, and other visual details, such as the bird's size (small, medium, or large) and specific markings and patterns that stood out on the bird's body (white eye stripe above eye, white wing bars on wings, dark stripe through eye, dark bars on tail, speckles on chest or belly).

Before too long, you may be able to identify a bird simply by its silhouette!

- Small silhouette (i.e., Anna's Hummingbird, American Goldfinch)
- Medium silhouette (i.e., Wood Thrush, European Starling)
- Large silhouette (i.e., Pileated Woodpecker, Great Horned Owl)

Promotes creativity, scientific knowledge, and observation skills

HELP ME UNDERSTAND

Q: Where does all of the information we have about birds come from?

A: Scientists study animal behavior, and the field of ornithology is the specific scientific study of birds. Information about birds comes from many sources: ornithologists, naturalists, birders, photographers, and people just like you and me, who take the time to observe and learn about birds and then share their findings.

11
......
ZOOM IN

FIELD MARKS are patterns, designs, spots, stripes, and colors on birds that humans use to distinguish one bird species from another. Birds use them to identify their own bird communities, too! Take your sketching to the next level by adding the field marks to your bird sketches.

Next time you're out sketching birds, pay particular attention to their field marks. Here are some things to look out for.

HEAD FIELD MARKS

Crown stripe (White-Throated Sparrow)—a stripe across
the top of the bird's head or crown

Eyebrow stripe (Carolina Wren)—a stripe above the
eye

Eyeline stripe (Chipping Sparrow)—a line through the eye

Throat patch (White-Throated Sparrow)—distinctive coloring
on a bird's throat

Eyering (Blue-Gray Gnatcatcher)—a distinct ring around
the bird's eye

WING FIELD MARKS

Wingbars (Northern Mockingbird)—thin, white or pale-colored
stripes across the wing

Wing patches (male Red-winged Blackbird)—blocks of color
on the wing

TAIL FIELD MARKS

Long tail—Brown Thrasher

Short tail—White-Breasted Nuthatch

Forked tail—Eastern Phoebe, Purple Martin

Tail with rounded ends—Gray Catbird

Tail with square ends—Eastern Kingbird

Upward-pointing tail—Carolina Wren

Downward-pointing tail—Northern Cardinal

Spots, stripes, or a coloration different from the bird's body—
Spotted Towhee

Cone-shaped beaks (northern cardinal, American goldfinch)—strong, cone-shaped beaks ideal for cracking open seeds

Long beaks (egrets, herons)—long and pointed for spearing fish and frogs

Petite beaks (warblers)—pointy and narrow for grabbing bugs off of leaves

Flat beaks (flycatchers)—flat and wide at the base for catching bugs in mid air

Spatulate beaks (spoonbills)—spoon-like for moving through mud and water to catch fish and crustaceans

Hook beaks (hawks)—for flesh tearing

Chisel beaks (woodpeckers)—for boring holes in wood and to search crevices for bugs

Prying beaks (crossbills)—specific for prying apart pine cone scales to get at pine cone seeds

Probing beaks (hummingbirds)—for drinking deep into tube-shaped flowers and catching small bugs.

• •

✔ *Promotes attention to detail, observation, creativity, and scientific knowledge*

HELP ME UNDERSTAND

Q: Do all birds have feathers?

A: Yes, all birds have feathers. They are the only living animal on our planet with feathers. That makes them pretty special, don't you think?

12

......

FEATHERED FIRSTS

IT IS ALWAYS EXCITING to notice a bird species you've never seen before. It's a feeling not unlike, perhaps, spying a unicorn in the woods or a mermaid out at sea—there's something mysterious and unknown that you've never seen before, and then suddenly, you see it. Even more wonderful is that spotting a new bird species may happen anywhere: in your own yard, on your way to school, through a car or bus window, while walking or bike riding, in your community, or during family travels!

As you and your child practice close observation of your outside environment, you'll certainly notice *resident* bird species—those that live in your area year-round. Many will be familiar and common. But every now and again, you will spy a species and wonder, *what is that bird? I've never seen it before!* It becomes a feathered first, and the fun begins as you and your child attempt to identify it.

You may also discover a common species with unusual markings, such as a *leucistic* bird—a bird with predominantly white feathers where the standard brown, blue, red, or yellow plumage should appear.

During migration seasons, you may discover a variety of species passing through or many new species that may even stick around for the season. On occasion, a bird species that is very far away from its usual habitat may appear in your area as a vagrant, or accidental, visitor. This happens for a variety of reasons. A storm might force a flying bird off of its regular migratory route, and the exhausted bird may need to rest far from its range. Juvenile birds making their first migration may miss their destination, overshooting or undershooting where they're supposed to be. And those who study birds believe that some birds may even be wanderers. Just as some humans have a tendency to wander, birds may do the same—perhaps in search of better food sources and habitat.

It's always exciting to see a new and unusual species, and it's always a thrill to see a "first"!

TAKE NOTE

Document the bird species you and your child see for the first time ever in your lives. Many birders keep track of each bird species they've seen for the first time and have positively identified, and these bird species are called *lifers*—meaning a bird that you properly identify and see for the first time in your life.

Once you begin noting all of the new-to-you bird species, you will be surprised at how many birds you actually encounter. Note each new species everywhere you go: at home, away from home, during travels—anywhere!

Never-before-seen species feel like a special gift from nature, and with each newfound treasure comes the experience of elation and intrinsic joy.

LIFER LIST

Today, for the first time ever, I saw a:

Species: Species:
Location: Location:
Date: Date:

Species: Species:
Location: Location:
Date: Date:

Species: Species:
Location: Location:
Date: Date:

Species: Species:
Location: Location:
Date: Date:

Stimulates anticipation, excitement, goal-setting, and wonder

HELP ME UNDERSTAND

Q: Why do people make lists of the different birds they see?

A: Nature is very complex and diverse. Making lists and categories of the living things we encounter in nature helps us to better organize and understand them.

DID YOU KNOW?

A "Big Year" is an informal competition among birders to see who can identify, by sight or sound, the largest number of bird species in one calendar year. In 2016, Arjan Dwarshuis broke the world record for most bird species seen in one year (6,852 species), breaking the previous record set by Noah Strycker in 2015 (6,042 species). Strycker traveled across 41 countries and visited all seven continents for his Big Year quest. For more information about this competition, visit the American Birding Association website, ABA.org.

13
......

FANTASTIC FEEDERS

MAINTAINING BIRD FEEDERS provides you and your child with the opportunity to easily share your lives with the lives of birds, and right through the comfort of your home's window—a joyful and rewarding experience, indeed!

Find joy in every aspect of maintaining your bird feeders: the thoughtful planning of how and where you'll place the feeders in your yard; the maintenance of your feeders as you keep them clean and keep birds healthy; the reward of providing for hungry birds; and the thrill of observing and making birds part of your family's day-to-day life experience. Each experience with bird feeding is a gift from nature, and the bonus is that nature is brought into your home through your windows.

Experiencing bird feeders may take as little time or as long as you'd like—from just a few moments through a window as your family enjoys breakfast to a day-long experience as you and your child make time to observe, enjoy, and wonder out your windows anytime you chance to glance out.

TAKE ACTION

When establishing and maintaining feeders, consider an organized plan as to what food you will offer birds, what type of feeder you need, and where you will place it. For example, bird feeders come in many shapes and sizes to support a variety of food sources, and you can hang them from shepherd's hooks, poles, tree branches (although here they'll be prone to squirrels and other animals), deck railings, and windows. Here are things to keep in mind when setting up your feeder:

- Consider placing foods enjoyed by smaller birds, such as finches, in an area farther away from foods enjoyed by larger, more assertive birds, such as jays and woodpeckers.
- Implement a baffle on bird feeder poles to keep squirrels, raccoons, and other hungry, non-bird animals out of feeders. You'll find baffles wherever bird feeders are sold.
- Place your feeders where they will be safe from window collisions. Windows reflect foliage and sky, and many birds fly into them believing that's just what they are—open space. Feeders are safest when placed closest to windows—within 3 feet—or when at least 30 feet from a window.
- Place feeders near trees or shrubs, so birds may take refuge and rest when necessary, but don't place them within 10 feet, which may provide jumping off points for squirrels.
- Place hummingbird feeders in shady or partially shaded areas. This prevents the sugar-water solution from fermenting in the sun.
- Designate a dry, airtight place to store your bird food, such as a lidded tub.
- Regularly clean your feeders, especially after rain, which can cause seed to mildew. To clean, just scrub with a solution of 8 parts water and 1 part vinegar, rinsing very well and drying after each scrubbing.

- Certain bird species enjoy feeding on the ground, below feeders. Keep this area tidy, raking away soiled and old seed debris to maintain a healthy environment for feeding.

Note: From time to time, you might notice a finch at your feeder with red, swollen eyes. Unfortunately, this is a sign of an infection that may spread to other finches through a contaminated feeder. If this occurs, take your feeder(s) down, clean them, and keep them down for a week to prevent the spread of the infection. You may report signs of finch eye diseases (mycoplasmal conjunctivitis) at Project Feeder-Watch, through the Cornell Lab of Ornithology. With your feedback, scientists may track the spread of this disease, which is not contagious to humans but is to other finches.

TYPES OF FEEDERS

Finch feeder—sock feeder, mesh feeder, or tube feeder to hold Nyjer seed

Hopper feeders—for a variety of seeds, nuts, and fruits

Nectar/jelly feeders—for hummingbirds and orioles

Platform feeders—for a variety of seeds, nuts, and fruit

Stackable cylinder feeder—for stacking seed, fruit, and nut cakes

Suet/fat feeders—as the name implies, for suets and fats (cool weather only)—designs with "tails," or long tips at the base, support the natural feeding habits of woodpeckers, providing support for their tails

Tube feeders—for smaller seeds

TYPES OF BIRD FOODS

A diverse mix of seeds with other food options will invite the greatest variety of birds. Here are some ideas:

- Apples and oranges will be enjoyed by buntings, cardinals, catbirds, chickadees, mockingbirds, orioles, tanagers, and waxwings.
- Black oil sunflower seeds will offer the most versatility with bird feeding, as they are enjoyed by most birds.
- Dried berries and raisins will be enjoyed by bluebirds, mockingbirds, orioles, robins, and waxwings. Soak them in water overnight prior to providing them.
- Mealworms will be enjoyed by bluebirds, robins, and wrens.
- Nectar (4 parts water to 1 part sugar) will be enjoyed by hummingbirds.
- Nyjer will be enjoyed by finches.
- Peanuts (raw, unsalted, shelled, or in the shell) will be enjoyed by blue jays, nuthatches, titmice, and woodpeckers.
- Shelled corn will be enjoyed by Northern Cardinals, doves and blackbirds.
- Suet (during cold weather) will be enjoyed by bluebirds, buntings, cardinals, chickadees, creepers, goldfinches, grosbeaks, nuthatches, tanagers, titmice, warblers, woodpeckers, and wrens.

* *

Fosters stewardship, responsibility, and an opportunity to learn more about birds

Q: Why do we see just the same types of birds at our bird feeders over and over again?

A: Many common birds visit bird feeders. This is a great thing, because when we become truly familiar with the ordinary, it provides us an opportunity to notice the extraordinary: we may then begin to notice a bird's unique personality and behavior. And we become skilled and ready to notice when a mysterious species happens by.

DID YOU KNOW?

The House Finch originated in the western United States and Mexico. However, in 1940 a small number of them were turned loose on Long Island, New York, following failed attempts to sell these "Hollywood finches" as pets in cages. Since that release, they have reproduced and their numbers have spread across the United States and southern Canada.

14

. . . . . .

GETTING TO KNOW YOU

IT TAKES TIME to get to know birds, just as it takes time to get to know people. Once you start to really pay attention—to notice and *encounter* birds—you'll see that certain species have very distinct personalities. Explain to your child that just as people have different personalities or behaviors—some people are shy, some people are bold, some people are silly—birds have different personalities, too.

Blue jays tend to be bold and boisterous. Wrens are the cats of the bird world, ever-curious about every little thing, inquisitive, cheery, and tenacious. Leave a window, garage door, or house door open? You can bet a wren will explore the open space. One pair built their nest inside my sister's kitchen. Remarkably, she kindly left her back door open for a month so the parents could come and go as needed to find food (bugs) and feed their nestlings, which hatched and fledged and were soon shooed back outdoors. That's what happens when you leave a door open in the spring with wrens around. Lesson learned.

And personalities even vary among specific species: one White-Breasted Nuthatch may be passive, while another may be aggressive. One blue jay may be courageous, while another is more timid. Birds strive to obtain the very same things we do: food, shelter, and a safe place to raise their families. We coexist, birds and people. Yet, when we have intimate encounters with birds, it gives us insight into the workings of the world and humbles us.

OBSERVE

Get to know the inner lives of birds. Become familiar with their behavior. Make time for little pauses in your day-to-day doings with your child so you may observe and experience birds around you, and these little pauses will provide a huge reward as you glimpse into their inner lives. Look for these personality traits and behaviors in birds:

- A bird that exhibits curiosity (exploring)
- A bird that exhibits affection (courtship behavior, mutual preening, sharing food, caring for young)
- A bird that exhibits fear (quick flight and escape, or freezing in place with wide eyes)
- A bird that exhibits aggression or assertiveness (posturing to chase away another bird; hissing at, lunging at, or diving at another bird)
- A bird that shares with another bird (sharing food or sharing space at a feeder)
- A bird that warns of danger (alarm or distress call)
- A bird interacting with another bird (chattering, mutual preening, or simple camaraderie of flying and feeding together)
- A bird that appears sad, lost, or ill (looking for a lost mate or chick, making a cry hoping for a response, appearing listless and droopy)
- A bird that is sleepy or tired (resting with eyes closed, bill tucked into feathers)
- A bird that is relaxed (often making purring sounds;

may sun itself, wings out and relaxed, feeling safe and non-threatened)

- A bird that communicates with another bird (calling to share news of food)
- A bird that is playful (toying with leaves to make sense of its surroundings)

As you observe, before long, you will be fully aware of each individual bird and its distinctive and unique personality. You will know these birds and count them among your friends and, perhaps, even fall in love with one or two (or three or four).

As you become more familiar with the birds that you observe and the behavior of each, ask your child if he has a favorite bird, and why? Record or document your child's response. Share your favorite bird with your child, too, explaining what traits drew this bird toward your heart.

Promotes empathy, observation skills, and understanding

HELP ME UNDERSTAND

Q: Do birds have feelings?

A: Scientists (ornithologists) and others who study bird behavior believe that birds do indeed experience emotions. They feel fear, relaxation, curiosity, and excitement. Their range of emotions continues to be studied and questioned. As you watch birds and their behavior, what do you think?

15
. . . . . .

THE PERFECT PATCH

ORGING A CONNECTION to the natural world around us is vital to our mental and physical well-being. When we immerse ourselves in nature, we form an intrinsic stewardship and interconnectedness to plants, animals, and this big, beautiful world. What a gift to give our children! We become in tune with the network of energy between all living things: birds, bugs, seeds, plants, and ecosystems.

One meaningful and unique way to immerse yourself in nature and the birds who call it home begins with having a "patch"—a specific place, all your own, where you may "bird" each day to take notes and count the variety of species found in that specific patch. Every bird enthusiast should have a special birding patch, a place you can visit regularly, a place you may get to know better than anyone, a place to unplug, tune in, and enjoy immensely. A place that is completely yours—shared with birds, of course!

Your patch might be a specific space or area in your backyard, or any place you can visit with your child by foot or bike, such as a green area near your school's playground, a bus stop, or a city park. Any natural space or locale that might entice birds to visit will make a good patch for you and your child.

Once you and your child have claimed a patch, begin visiting and spending time there regularly. Bring a pencil or pen for field notes and dress comfortably. While at your patch, quietly observe. Carefully listen. What do you hear? What do you see? How do you feel? Most birds are active during the early morning and in the evening. Does this make a difference with the bird activity at *your* patch?

Now that you and your child have a patch all your own—and you may claim more than one patch in more than one place—make notes and sketches to document the birds you encounter there.

Patch location:

Date: Time: Weather:

How many birds did you see?

How many different kinds of birds did you see?

How many bird sounds did you hear?

Sketches:

Promotes environmental awareness, relaxation, observation, and auditory skills

HELP ME UNDERSTAND

Q: Some birds look exactly the same, but one is bright and one is dull. Why is that?

A: Sometimes the male and female in a species look different from one another, a term called *sexual dimorphism*. Often, the male is more colorful than the female. A male's bright color, or plumage, may help communicate to a female he'd like to attract that he is healthy. A female's dull coloring, or plumage, helps her to blend in as she incubates eggs on the nest.

DID YOU KNOW?

GISS is an acronym for general impression, size, shape. The more time you spend with birds noting GISS, the sooner you'll be able to identify species by a mere silhouette, shape, flight pattern, or behavior pattern.

16

......

RAINDROP CAFE

RAINY DAYS BECKON EXPLORATION! Everything is washed, fresh, clean, and dewy. The air smells moist and alive with new scents. Water drops pool and glisten. Puddles form. Just as rain is often a welcome gift for our gardens, landscapes, and water sources, birds celebrate rain, as well. They rely solely on nature for the water they need to survive.

Head outdoors with your child following a rainstorm,

specifically to observe birds as they relish in all the needed moisture that nature has just given them. Find a spot where you can observe birds in action, such as on a deck or porch. If it's too rainy to be outside, you can also observe birds through a window.

OBSERVE

Can you find these rainy-day bird behaviors?

- A bird sipping from a shallow puddle on a deck, porch, or sidewalk
- A bird drinking from a puddle on the ground
- A bird drinking water droplets from a leaf
- A bird bathing in a puddle
- A bird bathing in water droplets on a leaf (hummingbirds love to do this!)

* *

Promotes awareness, understanding, and empathy

HELP ME UNDERSTAND

Q: Where do birds go while it's raining?

A: Although birds are pretty waterproof, birds avoid flying during big rainstorms, and do their best to hunker down and perch out of the rain under foliage. This is because storms make it difficult for flight to take place.

17
· · · · · ·

A HAVEN FOR
HUMMINGBIRDS

HERE MAY NOT BE a more welcome bird any-where in the world than the hummingbird. Wee wisps of air, buzzing wings, sparkling eyes, and a brilliant rainbow of iridescent feathers—they fill us with wonder and delight as they capture our hearts.

Hummingbirds can hover, fly backward or forward, and dazzle us, not only in their appearance but also with their precise aerial acrobatic capabilities. Approximately one dozen hummingbird species summer in the United States, with the most common being the Ruby-Throated, the Black-Chinned, the Anna's, and the Rufous. On the Pacific Coast, Gulf Coast, and in the Southwest, lucky you, hummingbird season is year-round!

As migrators, their arrival each spring is highly anticipated. And their departure, come fall, can often leave us feeling a bit sad as we worry over their long journey south. Many migrate thousands of miles each spring and fall. Can you imagine such a huge journey for such a tiny bird through the elements it may encounter: storms, predation, avoiding impact on human structures, navigating correctly, the Ruby-Throated flying over the Gulf nonstop with nowhere to rest, and the like?

TAKE ACTION

You and your child may create a safe haven for these wondrous jewels right in your own backyard, to welcome them home come spring. Once they locate the shelter and food sources you've provided, they will remember this haven and return to it year after year during each spring migration!

1. Integrate colorful, nectar-rich plants, either in pots or planted in the ground. Hummingbirds enjoy nectaring from tube-shaped flowers. Check with a local nursery or field guide for your region to find native plants that hummingbirds love, such as:
   - Varieties of beebalm (*Monarda fistulosa, M. citriodora, M. didyma, M. punctata*)

- Trumpet honeysuckle (*Lonicera sempervirens*)
- Cardinal flower (*Lobelia cardinalis*)
- Sage (*Salvia* species)

2. Place hummingbird nectar feeders in your yard or on your porch or patio, perhaps even adjacent to the flowers you've planted for them. Select areas that are shaded, or at least not in direct sunlight, so the nectar won't get too hot and ferment/spoil. Don't place more than one hummingbird feeder in the same area, as hummingbirds become territorial once they've secured a food source. You'll notice, once a food source is secured, one hummingbird will perch and watch over this food source, guarding it from other hummingbirds. Hummingbird feeders can be decorative, but be sure to select a feeder that:
   - Is easy to clean
   - Will not drip
   - Is easy to fill
   - Has an ant mote—a reservoir that may be filled with water to keep hungry ants at bay (ant motes may also be purchased separately)

3. Fill your feeder with homemade nectar (see the recipe below). Take your hummingbird feeder down and clean it at least twice a week, using warm water and a spoonful of white vinegar, rinsing very thoroughly with each cleaning. Use a clean toothbrush to scrub your feeder's sipping portals where mildew may grow. Use a bottlebrush to clean the interior reservoir. With each cleaning, replenish the feeder with fresh nectar, as sugar-water nectar ferments and spoils in the heat after a few days. This is part of the fun, the joy, and the process of providing for and caring for hummingbirds!

HUMMINGBIRD NECTAR RECIPE

Mix 1 cup of sugar with 4 cups of water (or 1 part sugar to 4 parts water for a smaller or larger portion). That's it! Here are some tips:

- Warm all or some of the water on the stove before adding the sugar. Stir the sugar in until it dissolves.
- Do not use honey, brown sugar, artificial sweeteners, or red dye.
- It is absolutely *not* necessary to add food coloring to hummingbird nectar. Not only is it unnecessary, it's not healthy for hummingbirds. Humans don't care for artificial coloring in their food sources. Why supply these wee birds with concentrated, artificial color?
- Allow the nectar to cool before placing it in the feeder.
- Store unused nectar in a lidded glass jar in the refrigerator for up to one week. A large mason jar works well, or a clean glass milk jug works, too.
- If you live in a region where species only breed for the summer, keep your hummingbird feeders fresh, filled, and available through October. Weary migrants may rely on your feeder as they travel through, even though they're few and far between in late fall.

✓ *Encourages stewardship and responsibility while fostering wonder and joy*

HELP ME UNDERSTAND

Q: Do hummingbirds only drink sugar water?

A: Hummingbirds need protein and eat small bugs, such as gnats, which they catch in mid-air. Bugs, along with sugar water and nectar from flowers, provide them with the energy they need to survive through each day.

DID YOU KNOW?

Hummingbirds must eat every ten to fifteen minutes and visit between one thousand and two thousand flowers a day. At night, hummingbirds go into a state of torpor, or deep sleep, where their metabolic rate is slowed by as much as 95 percent, so as to not consume too much energy while sleeping.

18

· · · · · ·

BOUNTIFUL
BIRDSCAPE

DISCUSS WITH YOUR CHILD the essential elements your family needs to be comfortable, safe,
and healthy: a home that offers shelter and protection, food, and water. Explain that birds require the same
things to survive in the wild.

Together, explore your outdoor space and determine if
it is a welcoming place that birds may inhabit and feel safe
and protected in. Like all wild animals, birds require food,
shelter, water, and a place to raise their young. These four
components help make a happy, healthy bird habitat.

It's easy to create a birdscape: a welcoming and healthy
habitat for birds. The birds will be rewarded with a safe,
nourishing haven, and you and your child will be rewarded
with their presence and knowing you've made improve-
ments to the environment.

TAKE ACTION

Creating a birdscape helps implement an ecosystem that
supports the health and livelihood of many living things,
which, in turn, supports birds. To feed the birds is to also
feed the bugs! Most North American birds—96 percent
of them (excluding seabirds)—feed their young insects

and arachnids. There must be a chain of life present in a healthy birdscape; the more diverse, the better.

1. Start small. Work with tiny patches outside your home to integrate native plant species into existing garden areas. Even pots with native plants on decks, porches, terraces, and patios will be beneficial.

2. Integrate native bushes and trees that provide berries. Not only are the berries an important food source for wildlife, but their flowers provide a vital food source for nectar-feeding insects, while their structure provides shelter and nesting spaces for a host of wildlife. Consider these species if native to your area:

   - Alternate-leaf dogwood
   - Arrowwood
   - Blueberry
   - Chokeberry
   - Deerberry
   - Bilberry
   - Elderberry
   - Hawthorn
   - Spicebush
   - Virginia creeper
   - Winterberry

3. Feed the butterflies, bees, and moths with native plants, and you also create a haven for toads, spiders, and other hoppy, creepy crawlies, which birds will love. Plants native to your area may include:

   - Beebalm
   - Black-eyed Susan
   - Cardinal flower
   - Goldenrod

- Joe-pye weed (requires a lot of space)
- Milkweed
- Sage

4. Avoid use of fertilizers and pesticides. Birds need bugs, as do toads and other wildlife. Allow birds and their wild friends to be your natural exterminators.
5. Implement a water feature: a birdbath, bubbler, or fountain.
6. Include evergreens, either planted in the ground or as shrubs in pots. Evergreens, such as junipers, provide birds with protective shelter year-round.

Bit by bit, piece by piece, as you and your child enhance your outdoor space with native plants, you will be inviting a host of wildlife, including your bird friends. Take joy in your efforts as you experience a growing diversity of wildlife right in your own backyard.

· ·

✔ *Facilitates stewardship, outdoor exercise, and living in harmony with the environment*

HELP ME UNDERSTAND

Q: What are native plants?

A: Native plants are plants that occur naturally in our area, having existed in the natural landscape for many, many years. They are part of our region's ecosystem; they depend on the wildlife in our area, and the wildlife depend on them, too.

19
• • • • • •
WING IT!

WHEN WE THINK OF BIRDS, we can't help but think of flight. And when we think of flight, wings come to mind, of course! Birds are masters of the sky, indeed.

Flight patterns vary by species, as do the shapes, styles, and markings of bird wings. Each type of wing has evolved with a specific function to aid in a species' survival. Explore flight and bird physiology with your child, and your child will certainly soar to new heights with wonder and amazement regarding these winged wonders.

OBSERVE

Take a moment to watch a bird in flight with your child, perhaps outdoors or through a window. Explain to your child that our arms are similar to a bird's wings. We both have an upper arm bone that connects to a shoulder. We both have elbows. We both have a forearm. And we both have wrists that connect our forearms to our hands—although a bird's hand is a bit different than ours. A bird's upper arm and forearm make up the section of wing close to its body, its inner wing. The remainder of the wing, the outer portion from the wing's center to the wing's tip, makes up the hand section.

Some birds (like eagles and hawks) soar with passive, soaring wings. Some birds (the Laysan Albatross, for example) have active soaring wings—these are long and narrow and use wind currents, which allows them to soar for a long time. Some birds (swifts and terns) have high-speed wings, which are long and thin and make these birds very

BIRD SPECIES	WING BEATS PER 10 SECONDS
American Crow	20 wing beats
Pigeon	30 wing beats
Chickadee	70 wing beats
Hummingbird	700 wing beats

fast. Some birds (cardinals or the American Robin, for example) have elliptical wings, which are perfect for fast take off and short, quick bursts of speed, but the speed is not maintained. Some wings are tiny and very fast—hovering wings—such as those found on a hummingbird.

Encourage your child to hold his arms out like bird wings. Invite him to flap his "wings" like a bird would, and practice flapping until his arms get tired. Then, using a timer—even just counting out loud will work—take it a step further and record how many wing flaps your child can make within a ten-second time span. Finally, compare his results to the birds listed on the previous page.

It's quite remarkable to think about the strength and stamina many birds exhibit with their wings! To wrap up this exercise, relax by reading an engaging children's book aloud together, such as *Animals in Flight*, by Steve Jenkins.

Facilitates exercise, empathy, and appreciation

HELP ME UNDERSTAND

Q: Are wings used just for flying?

A: All birds have wings, and most birds (excluding penguins and emus, among others) use them to fly. Birds may also use their wings to attract a mate, shelter chicks to keep them warm and protected, serve as a decoy to appear injured (to lure a predator away from a nest or chicks), and to cover captured prey, as an owl may do.

20
· · · · · ·

HATS OFF TO HUMMINGBIRDS!

SUMMER IS LEAFY and sunny and rich with plants, bugs, and birds—especially hummingbirds! They seem to be everywhere, flitting through gardens and visiting hummingbird feeders placed out for them. They're a joy to observe in action. So tiny, so quick, so delicate and full of detail. There are many fabulous things about hummingbirds—their remarkable migration journey each spring and fall, the female's cup-shaped nest-building integrated with spider's web, their ability to hover, and also the fact that they're a species that isn't too shy when humans are present.

With summer and hummingbirds in the mix, it is the perfect time to create a hummingbird hat feeder with your child and enjoy the thrill of having these jeweled wonders feed right from atop your head!

TAKE ACTION

Feeding hummingbirds atop your head requires a bit of patience and sitting still—a fun challenge for your wee ones.

4 to 8 colorful silk flowers (from bargain store or craft store)
Scissors

Craft glue or glue gun/glue gun sticks

2 to 5 individual handheld nectar ports or "nectar dots" (one-hole feeder source)

Baseball cap or straw hat

Hummingbird Nectar (page 60)

1. Remove the stems from the silk flowers using scissors or by pulling each stem off.
2. Glue the nectar ports onto the rim of the hat, spacing them evenly around the brim.
3. Glue the flower heads onto the hat, arranging them around and near the hummingbird feeder ports, careful to leave each port visible.
4. Once the materials have set securely to the hat, fill each hummingbird feeder port with homemade hummingbird nectar. Be careful when holding the hat once the reservoirs are filled so as not to spill contents.
5. Place the hat on your head and sit outside, adjacent to where you normally keep your hummingbird feeder. Take your original hummingbird feeder down (temporarily), so hummingbirds will be encouraged to drink from their new food source—the hat on your head!

Once the hat is atop your child's head, encourage your child to sit still and patiently. As the hummingbirds begin to feed from the hat, you will hear their wings "hum" as they approach and perhaps even feel a slight breeze from their rapidly beating wings. Your child's first instinct may be to jerk away, but coach him into stillness. If your child feels hesitant about having birds feed from the hat feeder on his head, wear it first and allow him to observe this fabulous and fun experience.

Facilitates creativity, patience, and feeling amazed

HELP ME UNDERSTAND

Q: How do the hummingbirds know there is food on the hat?

A: Birds have amazing eyesight, much better than human eyesight. Hummingbirds use their eyes to locate colorful flowers that provide them with the nectar they need for energy. They have adapted to using their eyes to locate hummingbird feeders placed out by humans, too.

DID YOU KNOW?

The female hummingbird builds the smallest bird nest in the world. She gathers and weaves spider's web into the design, which helps hold the nest together and allows it to expand as her chicks grow.

21
······
SEED SORTING

BIRDS EAT a variety of foods, such as bugs, berries, and meat/fish, to name a few. And, of course, nuts and seeds are associated with birds. There are a variety of birdseed options available on the commercial market for purchase to fill feeders, not to mention you may even grow your own birdseed by planting seed-producing flowers that birds enjoy munching on, such as helianthus (sunflowers), echinacea (coneflowers), and rudbeckia (black-eyed Susans), among many others. So, who loves to eat what in your backyard?

TAKE NOTE

Perform an experiment with your child. Obtain a variety of seeds for birds, such as black oil sunflower seed, nyjer or finch seed, and safflower seed. Look at the different seeds, noting the shapes and sizes. Ask your child to contemplate which seed will be most popular with the birds you feed, or what birds might favor a particular seed, and why. Write down your predictions.

Then, fill your feeder with just one type of seed. Take note of the birds that eat that particular seed over the course of one to two days. After two days, switch seed types, and observe once more. Do the same birds or same types of birds visit the feeder? Is the feeder visited more frequently or less frequently than with the previous seed? After a few days, switch to a third seed type and watch for activity, noting bird traffic, types of birds, and their preferences. Ultimately, is there one type of food that most birds seem to prefer? Were your predictions correct?

If you have several similar feeders, you may place one type of seed in each feeder and place each feeder adjacent to one another. Take note to see which feeder is the most popular and which species eats the particular seeds you've placed out.

· ·

Encourages a sense of wonder, hypothesizing, and analyzing

22

• • • • • •

YARD MAPPING

REATE A YARD MAP WITH your child, documenting your landscape and the birds and wildlife that frequent it. If you don't have a yard, no worries! You can map any space: your deck, a patio, a balcony, a porch, or a nearby green space, such as a park or public area.

TAKE NOTE

Take a walk with your child through the space you will map. Walk slowly and quietly, observing and listening. As you observe, make note of your landscape, as well as the wildlife you encounter. Where is it shady? Where is it sunny? What plants live where? Where are human dwellings situated?

Observe the trees, shrubs, plants, and flowers. Notice their forms and their locations. On a blank piece of paper, create a map of the space, using loose drawings to designate shrubs, trees, flowers, water sources, dwellings (human and wild), bird feeders, open spaces, and more. It's your map, so be creative and document the things you and your child see!

Don't fret over perfection with your sketches. Use general shapes: circles of different sizes—smaller for bushes and shrubs, larger for trees; flower shapes to depict flowers; squares or rectangles to depict dwelling spaces, such as a home or deck or patio. If you hear birds somewhere, mark the location by drawing a musical note.

As you walk through your yard, use your map to note where birds and wildlife are found. Explore during different times of the day, and while doing so, pay attention to the bird activity at each time. How does activity vary from morning to afternoon? From afternoon to evening? On rainy days compared to sunny days? On windy days compared to still days? Is one area on your map more populated with wildlife (bees, butterflies, birds, squirrels) than other areas? Do you hear more birds in one area than in others?

To become part of a community of people creating sustainable landscapes for their yards, join Habitat Network, sponsored by the Nature Conservancy and the Cornell Lab of Ornithology. You can access map-building tools, create a digital yard map, learn about habitat, and talk and share with members of the community. Visit yardmap.org

· ·

 Encourages spatial visualization and organization, creativity, and observation

HELP ME UNDERSTAND

Q: Why do some birds eat off the ground, while others eat high in the trees and other places?

A: There wouldn't be enough food for everyone if all birds ate from the ground or if all birds ate bugs from the leaves of trees. All living animals, birds included, evolve to adapt to their environment so they have a better chance at surviving.

FEATHERY PHOTOGRAPHY

BIRDS ARE BEAUTIFUL, and there's an artsy sense of pleasure that comes with noting their form and composition in nature. More than just a pretty picture, viewing birds through a camera lens allows you and your child to capture details and behaviors that are often missed with the naked eye. Photos also give us a still image we can study, allowing us to scrutinize all the amazing details for as little or as long as we'd like.

Photographing birds will provide you and your child the opportunity to visually catalog the birds you've experienced throughout months, seasons, and years. These photos can serve as a visual photo diary of wonderful times and memories spent together in nature.

Photos can also help us to identify a mystery species. With a photo on file, you and your child may take your time examining reference books, comparing your images to those in books, not unlike doing a puzzle or playing a game. It's fun!

TAKE ACTION

Bird photography can be tricky, as birds have excellent eyesight and hearing, are ever wary of their surroundings, and are always on the move. However, great photos are possible with patience, practice, creativity, and planning before and during shoots. Here are some tips and techniques to get you and your child started.

- Seek out lighting with the sun at your back but projecting on the bird(s).
- Do not wear bright clothes; birds have excellent vision and spook easily. Try to blend in.
- Do not make sudden movements; if you need to raise your arms to capture a shot or make any movements, do so slowly.
- A backyard with a bird feeder is the *perfect* place to practice, and here's a secret tip: attaching a natural tree branch to your feeder gives birds a place to perch as they await their turn to eat and gives you a natural setting for your photo.
- Capture the eye; focus your camera on the bird's eye that is closest to you.
- Shoot at high shutter speeds; this will help prevent blurred images, as birds tend to fly, hop, and constantly move about.
- Enjoy and embrace the learning process; learn how to delete images that do not work; read photographer blogs that offer insight on camera equipment and techniques.

Encourages learning new skills and facilitates patience and creativity

HELP ME UNDERSTAND

Q: Do birds see colors in the world as we do?
A: Bird vision is highly developed. They can even see parts of the ultraviolet spectrum invisible to human sight.

HEAVENLY HAWKS

SUMMER IS THE PERFECT TIME to grab a blanket, find a soft patch of grass, and lie back with your child, daydreaming, cloud gazing, and spying the occasional hawk. You'll find these heavenly flyers high, high, high, up in the sky.

"Hawk" is a general term that describes the entire group of diurnal (active during the day) raptors. Raptors are birds of prey and include owls, vultures, and hawks (falcons, eagles, kites, buteos, accipiters, harriers, and osprey). Some hawk species migrate each spring and fall, and many find a mate and stay with that mate for life. Because hawks are diurnal, daytime is the ideal time to watch them in action.

OBSERVE

Find a spot where you and your child may lie down and relax, ideally with the sun behind you, making certain the sun isn't directly in your eyes. (Never look directly into the sun, as this could severely damage your eyesight.)

Once you're situated, relax and take in the bounty of blue above. Scan the skies with your child. Who can spy the first hawk soaring high above? What other birds do you see flying across the sky? How are their flight styles different?

When you spy a hawk, note the shape, or silhouette, of its body. Just for fun, estimate how far away, how high up, it may be. Is it circling as it soars? Another place to find hawks is atop telephone poles near open fields, where they often perch waiting to catch sight of a meal, below.

Often, hawks are identified by their flying silhouettes:

- Accipiters (Cooper's Hawk, Sharp-Shinned Hawk)—short, rounded wings and a long tail
- Buteos (Red-Tailed Hawk, Red-Shouldered Hawk, Swainson's Hawk)—long, rounded wings and a wide, fanned tail
- Falcons (American Kestrel, Merlin)—short, pointed wings and a short tail
- Kites (Swallow-Tailed Kite, Black-Shouldered Kite)—long, pointed wings and a long tail

For fun, you might sketch the shape, or silhouette, of the hawks you observe flying above. Or just relax and watch them as they soar. Suggest to your child that she imagine soaring with them. Imagine their view, what they see below.

● ●

✔ *Promotes imagination*
  and relaxation

HELP ME UNDERSTAND

Q: How do hawks soar without flapping their wings?

A: Warm air heated by the sun rises up from the ground and into the sky. This rising, warm air is called a thermal. Hawks use these updrafts, or thermals, to give them lift. They stay within these thermals by flying slowly in circles.

25

······

CHICKA-DEE-DEE-DEE

OUR EYES ALLOW us to see what's directly in front of us, but our ears can hear everything around us. That's a benefit when seeking out birds!

All birds vocalize, and each species has a unique voice

to call its own: they call, chatter, chip, peep, tweet, whistle, hoot, caw, and sing. They call to send out warnings to loved ones, and they sing to defend territory and to attract a mate. They strive to make their presence known, and because of this, birding by ear is a musical and fun endeavor.

You and your child may bird by ear anywhere, including your own patio, deck, or backyard. Beginning in your backyard allows you to listen for birds you may already be familiar with—and it's a wonderful thing to hear a bird and know which species created the sound. However, birding by ear need not be about attempting to identify each and every song or call made; it's also rewarding to simply listen to the nature of birds that surrounds us.

OBSERVE

Sit outside with your child and close your eyes. Listen for birds. Bird sounds are referred to as songs and calls. Birds emit songs to attract a mate or defend territory. Calls, which are shorter than songs, communicate a warning or a bird's location. Try to hear as many bird songs and calls as possible:

- Do you hear a long song?
- Do you hear a short song?
- Does the song change in pitch?
- Does the sound resemble or include a warble, screech, chirp, or whistle?
- How many beats or syllables does the song have?
- Is there repetition?
- Is the song repeated by the same bird, or answered by another from a different location?
- Does the volume change?
- Do you hear calls? Is there a response to the call from another bird of the same species?

As you become more skilled with birding by ear, consider making notes on what you hear. Take it a step further and attempt to identify what you hear.

BIRDCALL MNEMONICS

Often, mnemonics are used to identify birdcalls and songs, as their sounds resemble words in the human vocabulary, such as:

- *Birdie! Birdie! Birdie!*—Northern Cardinal

- *Cheeseburger-cheeseburger* (very fast, faint, and soft, like a whisper)—Ruby-Throated Hummingbird
- *Chicka-dee-dee-dee-dee-dee*—Carolina Chickadee
- *Drink your tea*—Eastern Towhee
- *Fee-bee*—Eastern Phoebe
- *Feeder! Feeder! Feeder!*—Tufted Titmouse
- *Oh, Canada, Canada, Canada*—White-Throated Sparrow
- *Sweet-sweet-sweet; little more sweet!*—Yellow Warbler
- *Who cooks for you?*—Barred Owl
- *You're pretty, you're pretty, you're pretty!*—Carolina Wren

As you bird by ear, you and your child may create your own mnemonics for the sounds you hear!

Stimulates the senses and strengthens listening skills

HELP ME UNDERSTAND

Q: How do birds learn to sing?

A: Songbird nestlings learn to sing while in the nest. They listen to the adults around them and then practice replicating the songs they hear.

26

......

BEAK BY BEAK

BIRDS ARE BIRDS—but they certainly can look very different from one another. Each bird species varies in size, form, and plumage, not to mention their beaks. Beaks come in many different sizes and shapes, and each is specialized in form and function for the bird that "wears" it.

Beaks help birds capture the food they need. Some birds eat bugs, some birds eat small mammals, some birds eat fish, some birds eat seeds, and others eat fruit and berries. Some birds hunt for food while in mid-air, some birds hunt for food in the water. Some birds gather from trees, flowers, or shrubs; others hunt and gather on the ground. The types of food that birds eat (and how they hunt for that food) are as varied as their beaks:

- Long and chisel-like beaks are perfect for rap-tap-tapping into a tree's trunk to find bugs.
- Narrow and pointy beaks, like a pair of tweezers, are perfect for snatching and grabbing delicious bugs—well, delicious to the bird, anyway!
- Hooked beaks are perfect for grabbing and tearing.
- Spoon- or shovel-like beaks are perfect for scooping fish and other meals from water.
- Sturdy and strong beaks are perfect for cracking nuts and seeds.

- Long—very long—beaks are perfect for dipping deep into nectar-rich flowers.

TAKE ACTION

Explore how bird beaks work in the wild. First you'll need some "beaks" to manipulate and some "food" to practice with.

BEAKS

1 pair of tweezers (grabbing and pulling beak—robin)

1 straw (sipping beak—hummingbird)

1 spoon (wading bird beak—stork)

1 clothespin (picking up and cracking open beak—cardinal)

1 toothpick—round works best, as it's stronger than flat (piercing beak—wren)

FOOD

Rubber bands or gummy worms (worms)

Nuts and popped popcorn (nuts and seeds)

Cookie sprinkles (ants)

Cup of fruit juice (hummingbird nectar)

A few grapes and/or raisins (juicy bugs)

A dish of water sprinkled with a dried seasoning, such as basil flakes (small fish; algae)

Invite your child to practice using the variety of beaks to eat the pretend bird foods. Experiment! Which type of beak works best for each type of food? Explain that a bird's beak helps it capture the foods available in the environment where it lives.

HELP ME UNDERSTAND

Q: Are beaks used only for capturing food?

A: A bird's beak is primarily used for capturing food, but think about this: a bird doesn't have hands, fingers, or an opposable thumb as we do. So a bird uses its beak to do many other things, too. Beaks can pick up objects and gather nesting materials. Birds use their beaks to groom feathers, a behavior called *preening*. Beaks are used as a defense against other birds or predators. Birds even use their beaks to build nests—can you imagine using your mouth to build your house?

FALL

27

. . . . . .

COLOR COUNT

S DAYS SHORTEN AND become cooler and the colors outdoors change from greens to gold, the world we know shifts to the fall season. But there is more than fall foliage to marvel at when venturing out in autumn. Bird plumage also changes in the fall.

Birds are some of Earth's most colorful animals. But come fall, birds big and small, dull and dramatic, offer even more to see. The variety of plumage includes mature adults (molting or not), immature hatch-year offspring, and migrators passing through—each with its own dress code for the season. This can make bird identification even trickier than usual!

For example, in the fall, mature male hummingbirds sport their full-color *gorgets*—the colorful feathers that cover their throats. Hatch-year, immature male hummingbirds may sport just a sprinkling of colorful feathers on their gorgets, which makes it fun and easy to personally identify them as they frequent your feeder or garden: *there's the immature male with just three colorful gorget feathers; there's the immature male with just one colorful gorget feather; there's an immature male with no gorget feathers, or is that a female? I'm not certain....* And the cheery, male American Goldfinch, with mating season over, will molt into winter plumage and turn a pale olive brown, which helps it blend into its winter environment. Come spring, he molts back to his bright yellow plumage, with hopes of attracting a mate.

TAKE NOTE

Flock outdoors and seek out as many varieties of plumage and colors as you can find. Use this checklist as a guide:

- A mature male hummingbird (full-color gorget on throat)
- A mature female hummingbird (no color on throat)
- An immature male hummingbird (just a few colorful feathers on gorget)
- A bird with blue in its plumage
- A bird with red in its plumage
- A bird with yellow in its plumage
- A bird with orange in its plumage
- A small bird with brown in its plumage
- A medium-size bird with brown plumage
- A black and white bird
- A bird with white in its plumage
- A bird with gray in its plumage
- A bird with white wing bars
- A bird with spots in its plumage
- A bird with speckles in its plumage
- A bird with distinctive black markings
- A bird with bands across its tail
- A bird with a crown stripe on its head
- A bird with an eye stripe (line through a bird's eye)
- A bird with an eyebrow stripe (line over the eye)
- A bird with a black throat patch
- A bird with a white throat patch
- A molting bird (mixed colors; dull plumage mixed with brighter plumage; feathers missing)

- A bald bird (often found on cardinals or blue jays in the fall)

Add your own findings here:

Promotes awareness of the environment and observation skills

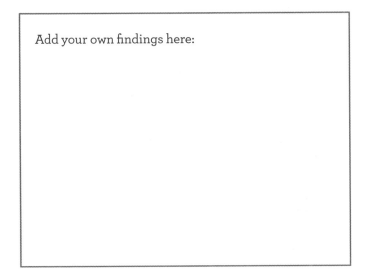

HELP ME UNDERSTAND

Q: Why do birds come in so many different colors, patterns, and designs?

A: Every detail in a bird's plumage serves a purpose. Birds use their colors primarily to attract mates. The markings and patterns on birds also help them blend in with their habitat, protecting them from predators or helping them sneak up on prey.

28

MOONLIGHT
MIGRATION

L EAVES ARE SWIRLING and twirling; pumpkins, hay bales, and cooler temperatures are present—fall is such a beautiful transition between summer and winter. It also marks another sensational transition: Each fall, billions of birds make their journey from northern, summer breeding grounds to southern winter grounds, where food sources are more plentiful. It's time for the annual fall migration.

Some of these birds are seasoned migrators, having made the journey before. Some of these birds are first-year hatch birds, having just left their nest over the summer—remarkably, they know where to go even though they are making the journey for the first time. Even the wee hummingbird that hatched over the summer will migrate, traveling alone, hundreds or thousands of miles, depending on the species. Songbirds migrate in the black of night, when there's less risk of predation.

Each fall also brings a Harvest Moon, a time when Earth's full Moon is closest to the fall equinox, and this marks an opportune time to go outdoors, commune with nature, and take in the mystery and wonder that is bird migration. The Moon provides a magical backdrop for watching birds migrate!

OBSERVE

Check your calendar to note when the Harvest Moon will take place, and at what time the Moon will rise. Plan ahead so you and your family will be ready for the timing. Invite friends to join you, too!

Gather together and head outdoors with a blanket for bundling up, chairs to sit in, warm beverages, binoculars, or a small telescope with 30x magnification. Simply direct your lens to the Moon. Before long, an occasional dark silhouette will be visible fluttering across the backdrop of the bright, silvery disc.

Migrators begin their flights right at dusk and continue until 2 or 3 a.m., with altitudes ranging from 1,500 feet to 5,000 feet, sometimes higher. Any full Moon in the late summer and throughout fall is an opportune time to catch this phenomenon.

• •

 Promotes relaxation, camaraderie with friends and family, and wonder

HELP ME UNDERSTAND

Q: How high up do birds fly when they migrate, and how far do they go?

A: Migration is not easy for birds, and the heights and distances they fly vary by species. Mallard ducks fly at heights of 21,000 feet, and White Storks migrate at heights of 16,000 feet. The Bar-Tailed Godwit reaches heights of 20,000 feet and also makes the longest nonstop migration, nearly 7,000 miles without stopping.

The highest-flying bird ever recorded is Ruppell's Griffon Vulture, documented at 37,000 feet where it, unfortunately, collided with a plane. The Arctic Tern migrates the longest distance, more than 49,700 miles a year, from its breeding grounds in the Arctic to its winter grounds in the Antarctic.

29

······

A HANDFUL OF
HUMMERS

BIRDS ARE VERY OBSERVANT of their surroundings, a trait necessary for survival. Even birds that frequent backyards and feeders are skittish, skirting and flying off at the first sight of human presence. However, certain birds, including hummingbirds, have become accustomed—wary but accustomed—to the presence of humans.

During fall seasons, hummingbird populations increase. Summer hatch-year fledglings are flying about with their parents in proximity. In addition, migrants from northern regions have begun their journey southward, adding to the population as they stop to visit food sources on the way to their winter grounds. Mature males travel first, followed by mature females, followed by the season's hatch-year juveniles who require more time to build fat stores before departing.

This population increase provides the perfect opportunity to practice proximity with these flying jewels. Invite a hummingbird to feed directly from your hand. If hummingbird feeders are already established in your yard, feeders will be busy with traffic during early fall, making it simple to get up close and personal with hummingbirds.

TAKE ACTION

To feed a hummingbird from your hand, obtain a handheld hummingbird feeder, such as the one made by Audubon, or simply hold the hummingbird feeder you have in your yard in your hand.

Temporarily remove any additional hummingbird feeders in your yard while you strive to feed a hummingbird from your hand, making your handheld nectar source the only source.

Make sure the feeder is filled with fresh nectar (see page 60), and place the feeder in the palm of your hand. Choose an area near an existing feeding space, where your hummingbird feeder once hung and your little jewels are familiar with. Then, sit or stand quietly and still with the feeder in your hand and let the magic begin. Hummingbirds may be hesitant at first, but with patience and stillness, they will trust you and the feeding source, and take a dip to lick nectar directly from the feeder you hold in your hand. Marvel as you observe the beautiful detail of their feathers, hear the hum of their wings, and even feel the wispy breeze from their movements.

Opt to not offer an open source of nectar, such as a milk lid or tiny dish with sugar water in it. If the solution should splash or get on the hummingbird's feathers, it may harden on their plumage and cause harm.

• •

 Stimulates affinity, wonder, and amazement

HELP ME UNDERSTAND

Q: How do hummingbirds hover?

A: Unlike most birds, which flap their wings up and down, the hummingbird flaps its wings forward and backward and can rotate its wings. This gives hummingbirds the unique ability to hover in midair, as well as to fly forward, backward, sideways, and straight up. In proportion to their body size, hummingbirds have very large chest muscles to aid in wing strength, and they have very tiny feet that reduce drag—a hummingbird can't stand, walk, run, skip, or hop; it can only perch.

DID YOU KNOW?

Alexander Skutch, the author of *The Life of the Hummingbird*, spent decades studying hummingbird behavior. After years of observation, he concluded that hummingbirds remember food sources, and perhaps the people who feed them. This is why, during migration, a hummingbird returns to the exact place where a feeder once hung, even if the feeder is no longer there.

30
· · · · · ·

LOVELY LEAF LITTER

WHEN WE CARE for others and foster stewardship for other living things, it provides the reward of intrinsic joy. When we model and facilitate stewardship with our children, we provide them with insight that will last throughout their lifetime. Simple projects in our outdoor spaces foster stewardship.

Working in the yard is heart-smart, too, providing fresh

air and exercise. In the fall, rather than blow and rake and tidy every little nook and cranny of your outdoor space, consider leaving the leaves—or some of them, at least—to create a leaf litter sanctuary, which avian wildlife will treasure.

When temperatures drop, bugs and food sources for birds drop, too. However, leaf litter provides shelter and refuge for bugs, which in turn provides important and necessary food for birds. The tidier the yard, the more barren it will be of wildlife, bugs and birds alike. It's as simple as that.

TAKE ACTION

Fallen leaves beckon. Get out and stomp and romp through them. Pile them up. Pick them up and look at them. How many different types of leaves have fallen around your yard? Sort and observe them with your child: by size, by shape, and even by color.

While out having fun, do you notice any birds scratch-scratching among the leaves? Look near hedges, a wood line, or areas that may be mulched. Create a tasty leaf-haven for wintering birds, using the leaves and sticks that have fallen in your yard. This doesn't mean you must leave leaves everywhere—just provide wee bits of habitat in place for bugs and birds to help get them through the winter. As you tidy your yard:

- Rake and place leaves and sticks along hedges, under bushes, and in mulched areas. Explain to your child that these are places where bugs may hide for the winter, and where hungry birds may find food.
- Rake and place leaves and sticks along fences, under

tree bases—particularly evergreens—and even over perennial areas, which will shelter *them* from winter.

When we get cold, we can layer in clothing or bundle under blankets. Leaves are nature's miracle blanket for the earth. They shelter, they protect, they decompose, and they provide nutrients for many living things. Birds love leaf litter! Look for these leaf-lovers:

- In the winter, you may spy Carolina Wrens investigating each leaf, White-Throated Sparrows kicking and scratching among the leaves, as well as Dark-Eyed Juncos, Fox Sparrows, Eastern Towhees, and Song Sparrows, just to name a few.
- In the spring, you may find Ovenbirds and certain species of warblers foraging on the ground through the leaves.

Encourages stewardship and fosters empathy

HELP ME UNDERSTAND

Q: Why do trees lose their leaves?
A: Winter trees "sleep" in a sense, and losing their leaves is part of their process to help them shut down for the winter. Winter days provide less daylight, and leaves need sunlight to function and make food for trees. Because of this, trees that lose their leaves in the fall (deciduous trees) drop their leaves as the days get cooler and shorter and then sprout new leaves come spring, when the days warm up and daylight lasts longer.

31

• • • • • •

HANDY NESTS

BIRDS ARE INCREDIBLE architects. Not only do they create the most diverse form of homes, or nests, of any animal species in the wild, but they create homes that defy gravity, resist weather season after season, and, most importantly, provide the perfect shelter and protection for their fragile eggs.

Nests come in many different shapes and sizes and are made from a variety of materials. They can be found on the ground, high in treetops or on skyscraper ledges, and even floating on water. Some are made of twigs, some are made of mud, some are made with spider's web, some with lichen and moss. Some are even made from bird spit!

In late fall and winter, you may spy nests among the bare branches of trees. During spring and summer, you might locate a nest based on chatter from a locale (hungry chicks at feeding time) or as you watch a bird gathering nesting materials as it flies to and fro. If you do encounter a nest, observe it quietly, carefully, and respectfully. Nesting birds need privacy and space. You wouldn't want strangers poking their heads into your home or bedrooms, would you?

TAKE ACTION

After exploring nests with your child, embark on building your own nest. Gather natural materials from outdoors: small twigs, sticks, grasses, and even mud. Then, use your bare hands to form and shape a cozy nest.

Is it a simple task? Can your nest support an egg? Survive through wind, rain, and other elements of weather? Imagine birds creating these structures using only their beaks and feet. An amazing feat, for certain!

As a follow-up activity and to learn more about birds and the types of nests they build, read my children's book *Mama Built a Little Nest*, illustrated by Steve Jenkins. In addition, visit your local nature center where your child may hold and observe a bird's nest up-close. Take a walk and see if you can spy a bird's nest—not easy to do during nesting season, as they're often well hidden. However, some species have the capacity to build their nests in the most unusual of spaces! Check out "Funky Nests in Funky Places" at CelebrateUrbanBirds.org. You may even submit your own findings there.

• •

 Stimulates understanding, empathy, and appreciation for living things

HELP ME UNDERSTAND

Q: Do all birds build nests?

A: Most do, but there are a few exceptions. For example, the Brown-Headed Cowbird doesn't build a nest. Instead, she finds a nest built by another species and lays her egg(s) in that nest, then flies off, leaving her eggs in the care of the birds who built the nest.

. . . . . .

A PUMPKIN-PERFECT
FEAST

PUMPKINS ARE SYNONYMOUS with fall, and thankfully they are ubiquitous at this time of year. Pick out the perfect pumpkin to create a "place setting" for the birds, a destination where they may dine on delicious seeds and nuts that provide them with the nutrients they need, while providing you and your little apprentice with a harvest-themed activity. Win-win!

TAKE ACTION

Visit your local farmer's market, or any place that offers pumpkins: a farm where you may pick your own, a local store, or perhaps you've grown your own? The makings for this fabulous pumpkin bird feeder are simple.

1 smallish pumpkin
Twine
A few small twigs, approximately 4 to 5 inches long
Birdseed

1. Cut the pumpkin in half, and then scoop out the seeds.
2. Cut two 3-foot sections of twine; hold them side by side and create a tight knot in the center, at the 1½-foot mark, knotting both pieces together.
3. Place the knotted part of the twine on the bottom of the pumpkin. Gather the four loose ends and securely knot them above the pumpkin.
4. Insert the twigs into the sides of the pumpkin, to serve as perches. Birds love to perch!
5. Fill the pumpkin with birdseed, then hang your pumpkin feeder from a shepherd's hook or sturdy tree limb, or place it on a deck rail. Just don't put it on the ground where feeding birds might be susceptible to predation by cats or other predators.
6. Sit back, relax, and enjoy the curious and hungry birds who discover this treat and come to feast.

*Promotes stewardship
and intrinsic reward*

HELP ME UNDERSTAND

Q: How much do birds eat a day?

A: A little chickadee may eat 35 percent of its body weight each day; the smaller the bird, the more it needs to eat relative to its body size. All birds must consume extra calories when temperatures are cold.

33
······

PRESSED LEAF
FEATHER ART

BIRD PLUMAGE IS AMAZING! Dots, stripes, feath-ery details, speckles, and spots. Feathers really are a work of art. Become inspired to transfer visions of feather design to your own feathers: pressed leaves!

TAKE ACTION

This is an amazing art project that you and your child may frame, scatter upon tabletops as décor, or give to special people in your lives.

Fallen leaves, gathered from nature (collect pliable leaves that are not dry or too brittle)

Opaque markers in various colors (black, blue, brown, ivory, purple, red, turquoise, yellow), available from any craft section/store

Fadeless paper (from craft store), for mounting leaves upon (optional)

Frame with glass (optional)

Craft glue, for mounting feathers on paper when framing (optional)

1. Press leaves within books and magazines for one or two days.

2. Once the leaves are pressed and dried, create simple designs on them, using bird plumage and feathers as your inspiration. Here are some ideas:

   - Create small, cream-colored spots across an entire leaf; then fill each spot with a small black dot, as you might see on the belly of a Northern Flicker.
   - Draw tiny "u" shapes and lines across a leaf, resembling overlapping scales, and then fill in each "u" shape with tiny lines that flow from top to bottom, just as you'd see up close on hummingbird feathers.
   - Draw small circles on a leaf, and then create small dots around each circle, similar to the dots found around a bird's eye.
   - Seek out images of feathers in books or online, and replicate them on your leaves.
   - Play with colors and design elements, letting nature and birds guide you in your choices. Draw the lines and details on these feathers.
   - Refer back to sketches you've made of birds, noting details in the plumage.

   Most importantly, be creative and have fun!
3. Place your pressed leaves as decorations on holiday table settings, or arrange them on fadeless paper in a design (star burst, array, single leaf/feather) and frame them.

• •

Encourages observation, fine motor skills, and creativity

HELP ME UNDERSTAND

Q: What are feathers?

A: Feathers are a very complicated micro structure of birds. They are so complicated and intricate in detail that scientists devote their lives to studying them: how they work, what they're made of, how they're structured, how they develop and evolve, and how they function. Feathers are unique to birds and are fascinating.

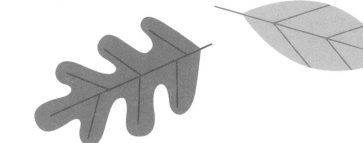

34

. . . . . .

SPEECH BUBBLES
BETWEEN BIRDS

AS YOU OBSERVE birds in the wild, do you ever wonder what they're saying? They sing. They call. They chitter. They chatter. Sometimes their calls sound cheerful. Sometimes their calls sound excited. Sometimes their calls are loud and alarmed. Sometimes their calls and songs sound extremely purposeful. Often their songs are melodic and dreamy. Just what do you think they're saying, anyway?

TAKE NOTE

One can't help wonder what birds are communicating to one another, but we do know they are communicating with purpose, just as humans communicate through dialogue, emails, text messages, and even through behavior and appearances.

Think about what birds might be conveying when they interact, and then have some creative fun as you ponder "bird talk." Peruse old magazines for images of birds, cutting out any birds you find. Glue each bird image onto paper, drawing a speech bubble above each bird's head. Then, let your child fill in the speech bubbles himself, or take dictation. Be creative. You don't need to be factual. Just have fun!

Encourages creativity, imagination, and fun

HELP ME UNDERSTAND

Q: How do birds talk to one another?

A: Birds talk using sounds—songs, calls, chirps, quacks, and drums—and the sounds they make are used to stay in touch with each other, attract a mate, contact a parent or mate, scare off predators, warn other birds about danger, signal a food source, or defend a territory, just to name a few reasons birds "talk."

35

• • • • • •

WE'RE GOING ON
AN OWL HUNT

BARE TREE BRANCHES and fall weather provide an ideal setting for spotting birds, and owls are no exception. Their silhouettes may be spotted anywhere you can find large trees, but it can be tricky to actually see them. Their plumage helps them to camouflage seamlessly with tree trunks, not to mention most species are nocturnal, or active at night. Don't let this dissuade you and your child from an owl adventure. Prowl for an owl. You may get lucky and catch sight of one or, at the very least, hear their haunting hoots and calls.

OBSERVE

Even though many owls are nocturnal, you need not venture out in the dark of night to find one. Dawn and dusk are great times to seek them out. They are active at these times, exploring their world, hunting for a meal, or calling to attract a mate or claim a territory. In early fall, you might spot owl nestlings out and about, testing and flapping their wings and testing their toes, climbing on trees.

Google owl species, and listen to their recorded sounds online for reference. Then, head to a locale where trees are abundant: perhaps your yard, a park, or a local nature center. Pack a blanket for sitting upon and a pair of binoculars, then plant yourselves down to relax, wait, watch, and listen. Owl prowling takes patience. But most importantly, you're making the effort and spending time in nature.

• •

✓ *Encourages exploration, curiosity, and relaxation*

HELP ME UNDERSTAND

Q: Are all owls nocturnal?
A: Of the approximately 222 owl species in the world, most are nocturnal, hunting at night, but not all. For example, the Barred Owl is active during the daytime.

BIRD BRAINS

BIRDS HAVE A LOT more going on in their wee heads than we give them credit for. (Just because they have small heads does not mean they have small brains.) They are smart! To the casual eye, they fly around, perch, seek mates, and forage for food. What a narrow view, though, in the scope of reality in a bird's world.

For example, some birds are tool users. New Caledonian Crows have been known to make and use hook tools, the only species other than humans to do so.

A young girl named Gabi Mann in Seattle began setting out nuts and dog food for the American Crows in her yard. They began bringing her gifts—toys and trinkets, pebbles, found jewelry, objects, and treasures—in exchange for the treats she left for them.

Each autumn, that little chickadee you see out and about is actually gathering hundreds and hundreds of seeds, hiding them in hundreds of places over 10 square miles—nooks and crannies within a tree's bark, under a roof eave, in a hole on the ground, in a crack on the sidewalk, within a tree's stump—and then is able to recall each and every hiding place come winter when food is scarce. And it does this easily, because each fall, the part of the chickadee's brain responsible for memory and spatial organization (the hippocampus) expands by 30 percent, providing it the spatial and memory capabilities of a brainy superhero. Come spring, when food is more plentiful and stashing seed sources isn't as vital for survival, the chickadee's hippocampus shrinks back to its normal size. These are just a few examples of the wiring in a bird's brain.

TAKE ACTION

Discuss with your child the many casual and common bird behaviors you observe: Foraging and feeding. Calling and signing. Wonder together: might more be going on than meets the eye? Explain to your child that chickadees have the capability to hide food in hundreds of places and then recall each hiding place when they need to access that food during the scarce times of winter.

Be like a chickadee! Provide your child with twenty-five pennies. Invite her to hide them throughout your house, anywhere she chooses, while you make note of each hiding space. Then, a few days later, invite your child to find all twenty-five hidden pennies. This is similar to a chickadee hiding seeds to serve as a food source through the winter.

Now it's your turn. Hide twenty-five pennies throughout your home—if your child is able, have her document each spot—then, a few days later, relocate each penny you hid. Challenge yourselves and increase the number of pennies you hide.

• •

 Encourages awareness, empathy, curiosity, and understanding

Q: So, birds are really smart?
A: Ounce for ounce, birds have significantly more neurons in their brains than mammals and primates. (Vanderbilt University, *Science Daily*, June 2016)

37

· · · · · ·

NAME THAT BIRD

WHEN WE OBSERVE and talk about birds, or any wild animal, they are often referred to as "it," as in "it" landed on the branch, "it" built a nest in that tree, or "it's" at the feeder.

However, seeing wild animals as individuals, and not just "its," can often prove better for the animal's welfare, while also facilitating empathy and forging a deeper connectedness for humans. After all, birds do not just exist—they live with inner lives, purpose, personalities, and emotions, just as we do.

Chat with your child about the names we give others. Parents name their children. People name their pets. We even give names to our stuffed animals and favorite toys. Scientists give names to birds, both scientific and common, to help order, organize, and classify them—necessary with over 10,000 species! Why not give names to the birds we learn to know and love?

TAKE NOTE

Give the birds you know names. They deserve to be named (and not just scientifically). After all, they share your home with you, as frequent or regular visitors to your feeders and habitat. Or maybe you notice a particular bird at a park. Certainly, as you become aware of the presence of birds, many become familiar to you, day in and day out, and display certain characteristics and personalities that will make naming them fun.

Any day is a perfect day to name a bird. Perhaps one day you notice a new species at your bird feeder, and she visits again and again. What should her name be? Or maybe you notice a guaranteed regular in your yard—a bird you see every single day, no matter what? What name shall he go by?

My bird friends include:

Name:

Species (my best guess):

Why I chose this name:

Encourages empathy and a connectedness to other living things

HELP ME UNDERSTAND

Q: Are there any famous wild animals that have names?

A: Many noted wild animals have been given names. Martha—a pigeon named after Martha Washington—is just one example. She was the very last passenger pigeon of her species, which is now extinct. In the late 1860s, passenger pigeons flourished in the wild by the billions, their flocks large enough to block the sunlight as they flew by. But in just a short matter of time, they became extinct due to over-hunting by humans and habitat loss. Martha was captured and kept at the Cincinnati Zoo with other passenger pigeons, where hopes of revitalizing her species proved unsuccessful. She died alone on September 1, 1914. Her remains are kept to this day at the Smithsonian Museum. Because she was given a name, it certainly makes her life and her life's story more real and relevant to us, don't you think?

38

CHILLING WITH FEATHERS

IN COOLER WEATHER, we often find ourselves bundled and layered, warding off the chill. Mammals in the wild may grow a "winter coat" to aid with warmth, while reptiles, amphibians, and bugs may burrow and nestle themselves out of sight until temperatures climb. But not birds. Birds weather the weather, thanks to their insulating feathers, which trap heat against their bare skin and keep them warm.

Feathers are not just for keeping a bird warm, and they're not just for flying, either. There's remarkable form and function to feathers. Here are other ways birds use their feathers:

- Feathers may help a bird blend in, or camouflage, with its environment, protecting it from predators, or allowing it to be the predator, unnoticed.
- Feathers communicate. A peacock may fan his tail to get the attention of females, a bird may "posture" and puff up to appear larger to scare off another bird, a crest on a head may be lowered or raised to communicate how a bird is feeling.
- Feather color may also help male birds attract female birds.
- The feathers on an owl's head help it hear by guiding sound to the ears.

TAKE NOTE

Take an autumn walk and look for feathers on the ground. Seek them out beneath trees, below feeders, or really anywhere, because birds are everywhere. Once you and your child spot one, pick it up and observe it closely, noting all of its details. Make a loose sketch of the feather. After close observation, place the feather back where you found it (collecting feathers is illegal).

With your sketches in hand, can you and your child identify parts of the feather? Each feather has a barb, a shaft, and a quill. Google "feather anatomy," or reference a bird book to study feathers in depth. The children's book *Feathers: Not Just for Flying* is a great resource!

Can you identify the type of feather you sketched?

There are seven types of feathers on birds:

- Bristle feathers are found around the beak and may be sensory while also protecting the face. These feathers are tiny and not ones you would find on the ground. However, you can spot them on birds you see up close, and on photographs of bird faces.
- Contour feathers cover most of a bird's body and give the bird its shape and colors.
- Down feathers are fluffy and close to the body for insulating and trapping heat.
- Filoplume feathers are stiff bristle feathers around a bird's eyes and mouth—again, as observed when viewing a bird's face up close or on a photograph of a bird's face.
- Semiplume feathers, a bit larger than down feathers, are also fluffy and insulating.
- Tail feathers are used for balance and steering.
- Wing feathers are specialized for flight; they aid with lift and moving a bird forward.

 Encourages curiosity, scientific knowledge, and observation skills

HELP ME UNDERSTAND

Q: We shower and bathe. How do birds keep their feathers clean?

A: Feather maintenance is important! Birds preen, using their beaks to go over every feather daily. They have a preen gland to help coat their feathers. They molt every single feather at least once a year. They bathe in water and even in dust!

A NEST OF MY OWN

EVERYONE NEEDS a place to chill and relax, a quiet place without interruptions. Even kids. *Especially* kids. It's healthy to provide our children with space where they can reflect, daydream, think, read, imagine, wonder, and simply be alone. Quiet time. No television. No electronics or other stimulation—a place to truly unplug and feel safe and calm.

TAKE ACTION

Find a spot indoors where you and your child may build a "nest," a cozy space just for thinking, reading, and relaxing—a nest your child may call her own. It might be a corner of a room, a sunny spot near a window, or even upon a sofa or cozy chair.

Once your child has selected the spot for her nest, provide a blanket or two and form them into a circular shape, similar to a nest but large enough for your child to sit in. Ask your child what else she may like in her nest to make it cozy: a pillow or two, a stuffed animal, or maybe some favorite books (some fabulous books about birds are recommended on page 171). Create the perfect nest, a nest just for your child to retreat into. Let your child know her nest is just for her to use whenever she feels the need.

Promotes relaxation, calm, and wonder

HELP ME UNDERSTAND

Q: Birds use nests, too—but do they use them every day, all the time, all year?

A: Birds only use their nests during nesting season for laying eggs and raising their young.

40

· · · · · ·

NAKED NESTS

THE WINTER TREE landscape is striking. As trees go bare, scenes that were kept secret by the thick foliage of spring, summer, and fall are revealed. We are greeted with new views and once-hidden gems: bird nests.

Winter trees offer beauty in their form and silhouettes against the sky, appearing both delicate and strong. Spend time observing the trees of winter and you'll notice a variety of nests—nests that were once snuggled tight and hidden safely within the trees' dense, leafy branches—are now visible to the naked eye. The diversity we observe with bird behavior is nothing compared to the diversity we find with their architectural nest-making skills!

TAKE NOTE

Take a winter tree walk, and seek out naked nests. Once you begin seeking them out, you'll see that they are visible in all sorts of places: within a tree's v-nook, perched high in a treetop among delicate twigs, within big trees, small trees, old trees, and young trees. Nests may be found everywhere during a winter walk.

Take note of the variety of nests you might see: large, stick-stacked nests, round cup-shaped nests, hanging pendulum nests. Pay attention to their sizes and shapes, in addition to the materials used. Look closely, if you can, observing each and every little detail. Can you see lichen and moss attached to the outside of one? Wonder about the bird that created each nest you find. It's tricky to positively identify each nest you see without its architect present, but knowing what bird species nest in your region, the location of the nest, and the type of nest can sometimes put a name to a nest.

Spend a day outdoors and sketch the nests you notice among the winter trees and their branches. If it's a sunny day, sit on the ground and notice how bright the winter sun is, as well. Without the absence of leaves and the shade they provide, the ground around trees becomes brighter, too.

· ·

Stimulates curiosity and wonder

HELP ME UNDERSTAND

Q: Do all birds nest in trees?

A: Many birds do nest in trees, but not all birds do. Some species nest on the ground, in caves, in chimneys, upon buildings (even skyscraper ledges!), and even on top of water, just to name a few places.

41
• • • • • •

FLAPPY HOUR AND THE GREAT BACKYARD BIRD COUNT

THE GREAT BACKYARD Bird Count (GBBC), facilitated by the Cornell Lab of Ornithology and the Audubon Society, takes place each year around the globe for four days in mid-February. It's a fabulous, feathery, fun way for bird watchers of all ages to observe the birds in their area, count what they see, report their findings as citizen scientists, and help create a real-time snapshot of bird populations—data which is instrumental to ornithologists and those who study birds.

TAKE ACTION

Partake in the next GBBC! Bird counting during the GBBC may be done for as little as fifteen minutes a day or off and on throughout a day. Simply tally the numbers and types of birds you see on one or more days during the count period. You may count birds at your home, at a local park, at school—actually anywhere. If you see a bird in a parking lot, count it. Just document the date, time, species, and place. The Cornell Lab of Ornithology has regional, printable checklists to use for tallying, as well as instructions and guides for creating a successful count. To get started, visit gbbc.birdcount.org.

Take the GBBC one flight further and host a flappy hour with friends and family! When we share our knowledge, passion, and enthusiasm about birds with other people, we expand the number of people who will know the joy that comes with watching birds. If each person inspired just one other person, the number of people who learn to appreciate the importance and beauty of birds doubles.

To host a flappy hour, gather materials for you and your guests:

- Bird ID checklists for tallying (printable from the GBBC site)
- Bird ID reference books featuring birds in your region
- A pair or two of binoculars (or invite guests to bring their own)

OFFER A CHALLENGE

Have a contest with friends and family during your GBBC flappy hour. Prize categories might include:

- First to tally the smallest bird
- First to tally the largest bird
- First to tally a bird (by sight or by ear)
- Most birds tallied
- Most species tallied

· ·

 Enhances observation skills and bird knowledge, and provides an opportunity to participate as a citizen scientist

Q: What is citizen science?

A: Citizen science is research conducted by people in the general public. By sharing their observations with real scientists, it provides a broader picture of the subject being studied and provides a wider range of data for scientists to analyze.

SOAR HIGHER

There are a variety of ways to practice being a citizen scientist. In addition to the GBBC, opportunities through the Audubon Society, the Cornell Lab of Ornithology, and the Nature Conservancy include:

- Bird Studies Canada projects
- Celebrate Urban Birds
- Christmas Bird Count
- eBird
- Global Big Day
- Habitat Network
- Hummingbirds at Home
- NestWatch
- Project FeederWatch

WINTER THICKET

IRDS HAVE different needs in the winter compared to summer, when temperatures are comfortable, nesting materials are available, and food and water are abundant—hence the reason so many bird species migrate. For resident birds who remain in the same region year-round, wintertime is a certain challenge. Water becomes frozen, food sources scarce, and temperatures chill down to the bone.

Create a thicket especially for winter wildlife to help them through winter's short days and long, cold nights. Although winter is not an opportune time to plant in the ground, you can provide sheltering landscape materials in the form of dense, evergreen shrubs in pots on your deck, patio, or throughout your yard. Come next spring, you can plan ahead and plant native, densely branched deciduous shrubs and berry-producing shrubs that will be a welcome sight for birds come winter. If you have evergreens in your landscape, leave the lower boughs and branches in place to keep them full, inviting, and cozy.

Leave an area with long grasses, instead of trimming everything down. This spot will provide a cozy retreat for birds when the weather is extreme.

Next, provide a brush pile of sticks, branches, and dried leaves in a quiet corner or near your yard's edge or along a fence, creating additional shelter opportunities for birds. Pile the branches loosely, with some edges poking out from the top so birds may perch and scan the area to make sure it's safe. Finally, install a "winter roost box"—a birdhouse birds may utilize in winter to escape cold temperatures and winds.

 Provides stewardship opportunities

HELP ME UNDERSTAND

Q: Birds' feathers help keep their bodies warm, but their feet do not have feathers. How do they keep their feet from freezing?

A: Bird feet do get very, very cold when temperatures are freezing. However, their feet are made up mostly of bone and tendon and have very little muscle and nerve tissue, which means they have very little fluid in them. This physiology helps prevent frostbite. Birds also alternate standing on one foot at a time, keeping the other foot tucked up into their bodies for warmth. Birds also have a "countercurrent heat exchange system" with their arteries and the veins in their legs to help warm the blood that is cooled by chilly weather.

43

· · · · · ·

TELLTALE TOES

WHEN SNOW blankets the world around us, it feels as if the whole world stands still. However, for wild animals—including birds—it's business as usual. There's food to forage for, and their foraging often tells a magical tale in the form of the tracks left behind.

Just who is out and about in the snow? Don't you want to know? Explore your snowy landscape and get to the bottom of the mystery. Seek evidence of tracks and tails. Look around trees, across open areas, near bodies of water, beneath feeders, bushes, and shrubs. Check near wood and brush piles. How many different types of tracks can you find? Use these clues:

- Are the tracks arranged in pairs with each footprint right next to the other? If so, the bird was hopping. Cardinals, chickadees, juncos, and wrens are hoppers.
- Are the steps staggered, one print a bit ahead of the other? This shows a bird who skipped along, such as an American Robin.
- Are there prints spaced out from one another? If so, this bird was walking. Starlings are walkers.
- Are the tracks found together, with multiple types along the same path?
- Where did they start and where do they lead? How do they vary in size and shape?

Have some fun and make your own tracks! Hop like a chickadee, skip like a robin, and walk like a starling. What other tracks can you make?

• •

Stimulates exercise, observation, and environmental awareness

HELP ME UNDERSTAND

Q: Are all bird feet alike?

A: All birds have four toes: three toes in the front and one toe in the back (ideal for gripping and perching)—but their feet come in different sizes and shapes, depending on the species. For example, a wading bird (think heron) has a very broad foot with long, narrow toes to give it stability as it walks in wet, mushy areas. Crows and starlings have much larger feet than the feet you'll find on a finch or a junco. Ducks, swans, and geese have webbing between their toes.

One variation to the "three toes in the front and one toe in the back" makeup can be found on owls, parrots, roadrunners, and woodpeckers. They, too, have four toes—but two toes are in the front and two toes are in the back, perfect for scaling and climbing surfaces. This toe formation is called *zygodactyl*. And all four toes on swifts face forward. Because of this, they don't perch but hang from their toes instead!

· · · · · ·

WINTER WREATH
FEEDER

MAKE WINTER—a time when food sources are scarce and survival is ultra-challenging—all about creating an outdoor space that supports and sustains birds. A winter wreath feeder puts a creative spin on the traditional wreath, and this one will hang sideways!

TAKE ACTION

This feeder is not only fun to make; it will also be a beautiful object that offers sustenance to hungry winter birds.

Jute or twine
Scissors
1 grapevine wreath (available at most craft sections/stores)
Aluminum pie tin or splatter guard (available from dollar stores)
Floral wire
Fresh pine greenery, trimmed from evergreens in your yard or from garden center shops
Dried bird millet (gathered from grassy fields or available where pet food is sold for birds)

Bird Butter (recipe follows)

Natural pine cones (gathered from nature, or store bought—
unscented/no glitter)

1 orange, cut into 4 wedges

Apple slices

Birdseed

1. Cut three strips of jute or twine, each 3 feet long.
2. Your wreath will be suspended from three points: 12 o'clock, 4 o'clock, and 8 o'clock. Run each section of twine through the grapevine wreath at these three separate points, knotting all six loose ends together at the top. You may also choose to knot the twine to the grapevine at these three points, and then gather loose ends at the top, knotting them together once more.
3. Poke very small holes into the pie tin, small enough for moisture to drip through but not large enough to allow seed to spill through. Poke two or three small holes in the edges, as well.
4. Place the pie tin in the center of the wreath. Using floral wire, attach the tin to the wreath through the holes poked into the tin's edges.
5. Add extra greenery pickings of your choice to the perimeter of the wreath by simply slipping the tips into open spaces of the grapevine.
6. Add sprigs of millet to the perimeter of the wreath.
7. Spread the bird butter into the pine cones' crevices.
8. Using floral wire, attach the bird butter–filled pine cones to the perimeter of the wreath, among the greenery and millet sprigs.
9. Using floral wire, pierce the orange and apple wedges, securing them to the perimeter of the wreath.

10. Fill the pie tin with birdseed.
11. Hang the feeder from a tree branch or shepherd's hook, and watch the birds enjoy the fruits of your labor!

HOW TO MAKE BIRD BUTTER

This recipe is a modified version from the Audubon Society (Audubon.org/news/make-your-own-suet). Note: suet recipes are not recommended when outdoor temperatures are over 50 degrees Fahrenheit, as the fats spoil in heat. You can substitute palm oil–free shortening for the peanut butter or mix it with the peanut butter.

1. Mix 1 part peanut butter with 5 parts cornmeal.
2. Toss about 1 cup of wild birdseed into the mix.
3. Blend the ingredients together with a large spoon.

* *

Promotes creativity and an appreciation for other living things

HELP ME UNDERSTAND

Q: Can birds smell the food we put out for them?

A: It was long believed that birds had a very poor sense of smell. However, scientists and researchers, such as Gabrielle Nevitt, a professor at the University of California, Davis, are proving past theories wrong. Studies are showing that birds smell all sorts of things. There's still so much to learn about birds!

......

DECK THE TREES WITH BOUGHS SO JOLLY

COME THE HOLIDAYS, keep little hands and little minds busy as they help deck the halls—outdoors. Find a tree or shrub outside that you can embellish and decorate with a variety of treats birds will love.

There are many foods and ways to create a holiday tree treat for the birds. Explore your outdoor area with your child, and select a tree or shrub that is easily accessible for hanging items upon. If possible, the tree should be visible through a window in your home. Here are just a few treats perfect for your tree:

- Using natural pine cones with open edges, coat each with suet or peanut butter, then roll them in birdseed. Use a chenille stick or strip of yarn to create a hanger by simply wrapping either around the wide end of the pine cone.
- Use natural fiber or string and non-sugared Cheerios to create a garland. Avoid using thin threads or fishing line, which may become a tangle hazard for birds. (This is a great fine-motor skill activity for wee fingers, too!)
- Pierce twigs or wooden skewers through orange slices.
- After snacking on an apple, save the core for birds— they'll enjoy the seeds! Attach a piece of string or a chenille stick as a hanger.
- Purchase small, ready-to-hang seedcake ornaments from your local seed store.
- Purchase suet baskets and suet cakes from your local store (available anywhere bird seed is sold) for hanging.

Once you've created and gathered treats for your tree, head outside and deck the boughs! Then, sit back and watch who takes interest in the tasty snacks you've provided.

Stimulates creativity and intrinsic reward

HELP ME UNDERSTAND

Q: How do birds find bird feeders and food?
A: Sight is the most important way birds find their food.

······

BIRD HAIKU

BIRDS HAVE INSPIRED humans for centuries in the forms of art, science, and engineering. Birds continue to inspire us to this day, keeping scientists curious, artists engaged, and people of all ages in awe, merely enjoying their day-to-day presence.

Writing, as an art form, can be a very challenging skill for children to master. It's subjective, and children often fear they'll make a mistake with spelling or grammar, which can block their creative process. However, if children embrace the creative part of writing and don't let the mechanics hinder their thoughts, they'll be well on their way to having fun with writing and mastering the skill. One simple, manageable—and beautiful—form of writing you may practice with your child is haiku poetry.

Haiku is a form of Japanese poetry that uses just a few words to create a sensory experience and vivid imagery in the reader's mind. Traditionally, haiku is written in three lines. The first line has five syllables, the second line has seven syllables, and the final line has five syllables: five-seven-five.

TAKE NOTE

Discuss with your child the bird experiences you have had together: bird behavior you've seen, species you've encountered, how birds move. Think of words that describe what birds do, like hopping, flapping, flying, feeding, picking, pecking, pulling, tugging, chirping (or, depending on the syllables needed for your poem: hop, flap, fly, feed pick, peck, pull, tug, chirp). Together, brainstorm meaningful words about nature and birds: trees, breeze, clouds, bugs, hawks, nests, bird feeders, types of weather, bird species, etc.

Using birds and nature as your muses, create a haiku with your child featuring anything avian. You might choose to write about a beautiful feather you've seen, bird flight, bird behavior, a specific species, a bird that captured your interest, or a specific experience you and your child have had with birds. Your child may practice writing the haiku on their own or dictate words to you. Collaborate!

Here's a sample:

Sunrise brings daylight. (five beats / five syllables)
A hungry bird looks for food (seven beats / seven syllables)
and then sees a worm. (five beats / five syllables)

Bird feeder with seed, (five beats / syllables)
one bird, two birds, three birds, four. (seven beats / syllables)
Time to fill again. (five beats / syllables)

Now, you try! Words do not need to rhyme. Just play with words and have fun with the process. It's a bit like a puzzle, getting the syllable count to fit each line.

. . . .

 Encourages creativity, applied knowledge, and writing practice

(five beats / syllables)

(seven beats / syllables)

(five beats / syllables)

Q: How long have people been depicting birds in their art?

A: The oldest art form featuring a bird is painted on cave walls of the Lascaux Cave in France, dating from 15,000 to 10,000 B.C. It features a bird-headed man.

47

......

SNOWY SNOWMAN
SNACK

A SERENITY HUSHES over the earth when snow
rests upon it, a quiet stillness as each unique flake
blankets the ground. We know that wintertime
can pose a challenge for birds as food sources disappear:
water sources freeze, bugs are out of sight, and plant food
sources dwindle. When snow falls, finding food becomes
even more challenging for birds.

If you live in a region that experiences snowfall, take advantage of this white bounty and build a snowman with your child specifically for the birds. Making your snowman will not only provide a much-needed break from being cooped up indoors, but your feathered friends will greatly appreciate this wintry feast.

TAKE ACTION

Build your classic snowman of three rolled, stacked balls. Once formed, embellish him with things birds will love to eat.

Suet or peanut butter
Pine cones
Birdseed
Sticks
1 orange, sliced in half
1 carrot
1 apple, sliced into wedges
Raisins
Flower pot tray (the kind placed beneath flower pots)
Peanuts in the shell

Get as creative as you'd like when making your snowman bird feeder, but here are a few ideas to get you and your child started:

1. Smear suet on and into pine cones, roll the suet-covered pine cones in birdseed, and then place these around the snowman's neck as a scarf.
2. Place two sticks or branches on either side of the snowman, to serve as arm perches. Sticks may also be placed on the snowman's head, as "hair perches."

3. Press each orange half into the face for the eyes.
4. Press a carrot into the face for the nose, which will serve as a perch to access the oranges, or use a pine cone covered in peanut butter, instead.
5. Place apple wedges on the face, creating a smile or mouth.
6. Insert raisins around the apples as teeth.
7. Place the flower pot tray on the snowman's head as a hat, and fill it with birdseed, peanuts in the shell, or water.
8. Finally, sprinkle some birdseed around the base of your snowman, for the ground feeders.

Encourages exercise, creative play, and stewardship for living things

HELP ME UNDERSTAND

Q: How do some birds stay where it's cold, not migrating to warmer places as other birds do?

A: Birds that remain in cold weather and that do not migrate have adapted to their environment. Adaptation means fitting in to survive. Birds that "overwinter" have adapted by switching food sources from plentiful insects in the summer to seeds and fruits on native plants in the winter.

48

·····

WINDOW TO THE WORLD

INTER DAYS can sometimes feel drab and dull, with cloud cover making skies and landscapes appear as one monochromatic color scheme. However, on days like this, birds brighten and pop in the landscape. Winter also provides additional viewing opportunities for birds among naked branches; come spring and summer, those same branches will fill with foliage and hide birds.

OBSERVE

Pick a particularly gray day to hunker down with your little chick near a window for a scavenger hunt. Make him comfy with snacks and a beverage. Explain that you're going to embark on an adventure through the wintry window to seek out as many items on the scavenger hunt list as possible. You may create your own list of items to find, depending on your region, but here are some ideas to get you started:

- A bird tucking one foot up into its body, to keep its feet warm
- bird hunkered down low on top of its feet, in an effort to keep its feet warm
- A bird puffed up, keeping warm
- A busy bird (what is it doing?)
- A perching bird
- A red-colored bird
- A bird with black in its plumage
- A black-and-white bird
- A brown-colored bird
- A tan-colored bird
- A black-colored bird
- A blue-colored bird
- A gray bird
- A hopping bird
- A bird scratching at the ground
- A bird feeding from a feeder
- A male bird with bright plumage
- A female bird with dull plumage
- A flock of birds
- A hopping bird
- A flock of geese flying overhead

- A bird with a crest on its head
- A bird with a long, pointy, bug-eating beak
- A bird with a triangular, seed-eating beak
- A bird with white wing bars
- A bird in a tree
- A bird species you can only find during the winter
- A hawk flying overhead
- A bird wiping its beak on a branch
- A pecking bird

Encourages observation skills and persistence

HELP ME UNDERSTAND

Q: I noticed a woodpecker with the side of his head up against a tree trunk. It looked as if he were trying to hug the tree. What was he doing?

A: Woodpeckers may place an ear up against a tree's trunk to listen for bug activity, to help them find a meal.

· · · · · ·

A BIRD IN THE HAND

IMAGINE BEING so close to birds that you can see every detail of their tiniest feathers with your naked eye as you watch them crack seeds open with their beaks— right on your very hand.

Sometimes we need an excuse to get out in the winter, and this adventurous activity is perfect for a day that's not too nippy—an opportunity to bask in fresh air and experience wild birds in all their glory. The primary goal is to get birds to land on your hand to eat seed you've placed there. Birds are so wary of our presence, and this sounds difficult, but it's not. (This activity is inspired by Jim Carpenter, founder of Wild Birds Unlimited, and his book, *The Joy of Bird Feeding*.)

TAKE ACTION

First, make certain you have active, feeding birds at your feeder.

Next, place a patio chair with arms near your feeder with a "dummy" sitting upright in it—the dummy being an empty jacket. Place a pillow inside the jacket to give it substance and help it stay erect in the chair. Place a hat over the jacket collar opening. Any type of hat will work: a woolen cap or a baseball cap. Place a glove at the arm opening of the jacket, palm upright, resting on the chair's arm, propping it near the feeder, and then place bird food (seeds and nuts) in the palm of the glove.

Wait an hour or two for the birds to become accustomed to gathering seed from both the gloved hand and their feeder. Eventually, remove all the birdseed from your bird feeder, but keep seeds and nuts in the gloved hand. Soon, the birds will discover that the feeder is empty and will continue eating out of the gloved hand, instead.

Keep the gloved hand full of seeds and nuts. After another hour or two, put on the jacket (or one similar to what the "dummy" is wearing), the hat, and the glove, and take the dummy's place in the chair. Fill *your* gloved hand with seeds and nuts, and rest it on the chair's arm. Allow your child to watch from a window, as you remain calm and quiet and still. Soon, the birds will be eating out of your hand.

If the weather permits, you may experiment with taking the glove off and placing food directly into your hand for the birds to eat. It's important to keep still, though. Once a bird lands on your hand, you may be inclined to jump or flinch or react—it may tickle or feel startling—but remain still and enjoy the wonder and awe right before your very eyes. Then, invite your child to trade places with you, taking turns so he may enjoy this remarkable experience.

• •

Practices the art of patience and perseverance; promotes wonder and awe

HELP ME UNDERSTAND

Q: Can't the birds tell the difference between the dummy and a real person?

A: Yes and no. Birds are smart and have excellent hearing and eyesight. Once they determine—through observation, listening, familiarity, and practice—that the dummy holds no threat to them, they determine it's a safe feeding source. As we take the place of the dummy and behave the same (still and motionless), birds ascertain that we are a safe feeding source, as well. However, any sudden movement on our part will have them taking flight.

50

. . . . . .

SURF, SAND, I SPY
A BIRD BAND!

WINTER IS A POPULAR TIME to escape to sunny, warm beaches—or perhaps you live near a beach year-round. Regardless of how you manage to spend time with your wee ones among surf and sand, next time you're there, make note of others who are enjoying the beach, too: shorebirds!

Observing shorebirds is a rewarding and relaxing way to spend time at the beach. It can also prove to be rewarding for the birds, should you chose to participate as a citizen scientist. As you pack your beach bag, include a field guide to shorebirds in the region where you are, along with a pencil and notepad and a pair of binoculars or a camera with a zoom lens. Then, be on the lookout for banded birds on the beach.

Shorebirds and water birds are relatively long-legged. As you observe them on the beach, you may notice a colorful band around one or both of their legs. Bird banding is an extremely valuable tool in the study and conservation of bird species. Bands may be metal or plastic and often will be marked with a code of letters and numbers unique to each bird. These "codes" will tell biologists where and when that particular bird hatched. Bands also help biologists track bird movement, migration, and mortality—a fascinating glimpse into a bird's life and history!

Spotting and reporting a banded bird is a wonderful way to be a citizen scientist, and biologists rely and very much appreciate when we take time to spot, note, and share a sighted band with them.

TAKE ACTION

Using your camera or binoculars, quietly and calmly sit nearby an area where shorebirds are resting or feeding, careful not to flush them into flight. Many shorebirds have migrated hundreds or even thousands of miles to the beach where you see them; it's important to allow them their space without disturbing them. Once situated near birds on the beach, quietly spy and look out for bands on legs. This can be a fun and challenging activity for your child!

Be sure to note the following:

- The location of the band. Is the band above or below the ankle (the ankle is the joint in the middle of a bird's leg)?
- The color of the band
- The color of the writing on the band
- The code, if you can see it; write it down, if you can, or document it with your camera
- The date and location of your observation

Once noted, report the band, even if it's just the color and location. Every little bit of information provided to biologists will prove insightful.

You can report banded birds using the following resources:

- Patuxent Wildlife Research Center Bird Banding

Laboratory, the United States Geological Survey: www
.pwrc.usgs.gov/BBL/bblretrv
- Banded Birds.Org: bandedbirds.org
- Audubon Atlantic Flyway: nc.audubon.org

Encourages environmental awareness, citizen scientist involvement, persistence, and observation skills

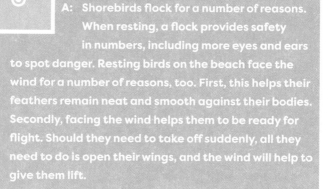

HELP ME UNDERSTAND

Q: Why do many shorebirds rest in flocks on the beach, all facing the same direction?

A: Shorebirds flock for a number of reasons. When resting, a flock provides safety in numbers, including more eyes and ears to spot danger. Resting birds on the beach face the wind for a number of reasons, too. First, this helps their feathers remain neat and smooth against their bodies. Secondly, facing the wind helps them to be ready for flight. Should they need to take off suddenly, all they need to do is open their wings, and the wind will help to give them lift.

51
......

NEW YEAR'S BIRD

HAPPY NEW YEAR! As you and your child embark on the first day of the new year, make it a point to wonder together what might be the very first bird you see on this New Year's Day.

First, make a guess as to what bird you might see. Then, wait and watch.

As you spy your first bird of the new year, rejoice! Then, give thanks for the many blessings nature gives us—and it's all free and right outside our doors and windows, just waiting for exploration.

Make spotting the first bird of the new year an annual tradition for your family, something to eagerly anticipate and celebrate. Wonder . . . what might be the first bird species you see the next morning, and the morning after that. Consider keeping track and noting any pattern to the species that you encounter for the first time each morning or day.

 Promotes enthusiasm, wonder, and excitement

HELP ME UNDERSTAND

Q: Will the first bird we saw on New Year's Day be the same species we see for the first time each New Year's Day?

A: The only way to find out is to observe, year after year, on each New Year's Day!

52

· · · · · ·

NEW YEAR'S BIRD RESOLUTIONS

THE START OF A NEW YEAR is always a hopeful time, with fresh ideas and new beginnings—and of course, resolutions to guide us along and kick-start the future. We can apply the same philosophy to our lives with birds in the year ahead, so why not make some New Year's bird resolutions with your child as part of next year's plan?

TAKE NOTE

With your child, discuss and reflect back on your life with birds. Then, envision how you'd like to experience birds in your lives in the future.

- Maybe there's a species of bird you've yet to see, hear, or identify?
- Maybe you'd like to better identify birds by their calls?
- Maybe you'd like to attract additional bird species to your backyard, increasing your yard's diversity?
- Maybe you'd like to travel to seek out bird species that aren't specific to your region?
- What about those elusive, tricky-to-identify warblers? Maybe this is the year to seek them out and practice identifying them?

- Maybe you'd like to volunteer at a wild bird rehab facility? Or give back to birds in some other manner?
- Maybe you'd like to foster stewardship for future generations and introduce a friend or other family members to the lives of birds?
- Maybe you'd like to join a bird club? Or better yet, form one!
- Maybe you'd like to read more books about birds to learn more about them?
- Maybe you'd like to connect with other birders in your community, networking and birding together?

Create your New Year's bird resolutions with your child. Then, reflect upon them and revisit them throughout the year. But most importantly, enjoy your love of birding and have fun together as you become ambassadors of joy with birds!

 Encourages goal setting and promotes excitement for things to come

HELP ME UNDERSTAND

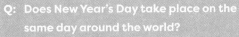

Q: Does New Year's Day take place on the same day around the world?

A: New Year's Day takes place on different dates of the year, depending on the country celebrating the New Year. However, regardless of date or locale, each New Year is one of celebration.

ACKNOWLEDGMENTS

I AM NOT AN ORNITHOLOGIST. I am merely someone who finds extreme joy in everything avian. Birds have become the sun in my universe; thus, my family and I orbit around their existence wherever we go. For this I am grateful for birds, of course, and bestow a heartfelt and loving thanks to my husband Charlie, who somehow manages to point out bird species I always miss. Loving thanks also to my daughter, Kelly, my sisters, Kristen and Debbie, and my main peep, Christina Kaman—for their patience, understanding, knowledge, and shared enthusiasm as we venture out in nature together.

I couldn't have published this book without the time and knowledge shared by the St. Louis Audubon Society. I am indebted to the folks there who poured over these pages to check my writing for ornithological accuracy. A special shout-out and thanks to Mitch Leachman and Pat Lueders. May I add, I take the sole responsibility for any scientific inaccuracies that may occur in the pages of this book.

Eternal gratitude to my parents, Paul and Charlene Sultan, for sharing the wonders of nature with me throughout my childhood and filling my world with books that opened and expanded my horizon even more. I love you both so much and am so grateful.

Deep appreciation to the wind beneath my wings: my

agent, Stefanie Von Borstel, for her never-ending cheer-leading with my projects; my editor, Jenn Urban-Brown, for her vision and patience with this book; and the team at Shambhala Publications/Roost for bringing this book to fruition—thank you!

Great respect and thanks to the many folks who have provided me with insight into the lives of birds, help with the writing process, and who share the joy of environmental stewardship—adventurers, artists, authors, book folk, educators, environmentalists, friends, naturalists, photographers, scientists, stewards—the world is more rich with your presence: Linze Aya, Ruth Beeker, Brooke Bessesen, Judy Boise, Loree Griffin Burns, Todd Christopher, Laurie Coffey, Susan Dierker, Cynthia Jenson-Elliott, Scott Evers, Denise Fleming, Candy Fowler, Greg Fowler, Lisa Fowler, Kate Garchinsky, Susie Ghahremani, Maria Gianferrari, Cindy Gray, Steve Gray, Steve Jenkins, Bart King, Lisa King, Teri Kingston, Suzy Leopold, Richard Louv, Sharon Lovejoy, Stephanie L. McAndrews, Alice McGinty, Kate Messner, David Mizejewski, Heather Montgomery, Robert Mulvihill, Diane Schneider Munster, Terry Pierce, Laurence Pringle, Sarah Schwartzman Palermo, Ann Pettigrew, Hob Osterlund, Russell Reed, April Pulley Sayre, Liz Garton Scanlon, Randi Miller Sonenshine, Sharon Sorensen, Melissa Stewart, Debbie Sultan, Kristen Sultan, Jing Jing Tsong, Deborah Vath, Kelly Ward, Tamra Wight, Sallie Wolf, and Julie (Never-Walk-by-a-Weed-without Pulling-It) Zickefoose.

RESOURCES AND RECOMMENDED READING

. . . .

BOOKS AND MAGAZINES FOR ADULTS

Ackerman, Jennifer. *The Genius of Birds*. Penguin Press, 2016.

Alderfer, Jonathan. *National Geographic Backyard Guide to the Birds of North America*. National Geographic, 2011.

Birds and Blooms Magazine

BirdWatching Magazine

Carpenter, Jim. *The Joy of Bird Feeding: The Essential Guide to Attracting and Feeding Our Backyard Birds*. Scott & Nix, Inc., 2017.

Erickson, Laura. *101 Ways to Help Birds*. Stackpole Books, 2006.

———. *Sharing the Wonder of Birds with Kids*. University of Minnesota Press, 1997.

———. *The Bird Watching Answer Book: Everything You Need to Know to Enjoy Birds in Your Backyard and Beyond*. Cornell Lab of Ornithology, 2009.

Heinrich, Bernd. *One Wild Bird at a Time: Portraits of Individual Lives*. Houghton Mifflin Harcourt, 2016.

Kaufman, Kenn. *Kingbird Highway: The Biggest Year in the Life of an Extreme Birder*. Houghton Mifflin Harcourt, 2006.

Living Bird Magazine

Louv, Richard. *The Nature Principle: Reconnecting with Life in a Virtual Age*. Algonquin Books, 2012.

Mizejewski, David. *National Wildlife Federation: Attracting Birds, Butterflies and Backyard Wildlife*. Creative Homeowner, 2004.

Osterlund, Hob. *Holy Moli: Albatross and Other Ancestors*. Oregon State University Press 2016.

Safina, Carl. *Beyond Words: What Animals Think and Feel*. Picador; Reprint Edition, 2016.

Sayre, April Pulley. *Touch a Butterfly: Wildlife Gardening for Kids—Simple Ways to Attract Birds*.

Sampson, Scott D. *How to Raise a Wild Child: The Art and Science of Falling in Love with Nature*. Mariner Books, 2016.

Sorenson, Sharon. *Birds in the Yard Month by Month*. Stackpole Books, 2013.

Stiteler, Sharon. *1001 Secrets Every Birder Should Know: Tips and Trivia for the Backyard and Beyond*. Running Press, 2013.

Stokes, Donald. *Stokes Beginner's Guide to Birds: Eastern Region (Stokes Field Guide Series)*. Little Brown and Company, 1996.

———. *The Hummingbird Book: The Complete Guide to Attracting, Identifying, and Enjoying Hummingbirds*. Little Brown and Company, 1989.

Stryker, Noah. *The Thing With Feathers: The Surprising Lives of Birds and What They Reveal About Being Human*. Riverhead Books, 2015.

Tallamy, Douglas W. *Bringing Nature Home: How You Can Sustain Wildlife with Native Plants* .Timber Press, 2007.

Young, Jon. *What The Robin Knows: How Birds Reveal the Secrets of the Natural World*. Mariner Books, 2013.

Zickefoose, Julie. *Baby Birds: An Artist Looks Into the Nest*.

Houghton Mifflin Harcourt, 2016.

———. *Natural Gardening for Birds: Create a Bird-Friendly Habitat in Your Backyard*. Skyhorse Publishing, July 2016.

FABULOUS BIRD BOOKS FOR CHILDREN

Aston, Dianna. *An Egg is Quiet*. Chronicle Books, 2014.

———. *A Nest is Noisy*. Chronicle Books, 2017.

Baker, Jeannie. *Circle*. Candlewick, 2016.

Bierregaard, Rob. *Belle's Journey: An Osprey Takes Flight*. Charlesbridge, 2018.

Cate, Annette Leblanc. *Look Up! Bird-watching in Your Own Backyard*. Candlewick, 2013.

Christelow, Eileen. *Robins! How They Grow Up*. Clarion Books, 2017.

Collard, Sneed. *Beaks!* Charlesbridge, 2002.

———. *Woodpeckers*. Bucking Horse Books, 2018.

———. *Firebirds*. Bucking Horse Books, 2015.

Davies, Jacqueline. *The Boy Who Drew Birds*. HMH Books for Young Readers, 2004.

Deacon, Alexis. *I Am Henry Finch*. Candlewick, 2015.

Dierker, Susan. *Albatross of Kauai: The Story of Kaloaku-lua*. Done by Dogs Publishing, 2014.

Ehlert, Lois. *Feathers for Lunch*. HMH Books for Young Readers, 1996.

Elliott, David. *On the Wing*. Candlewick, 2014.

Erickson, Laura. *Am I Like You?* Cornell Lab Publishing Group, 2016.

Fleming, Denise. *This is the Nest That Robin Built*. Beach Lane, 2018.

Florian, Douglas. *On the Wing: Bird Poems and Paintings*. HMH Books for Young Readers, 2000.

Franco, Betsy. *Birdsongs*. Margaret K. McElderry Books, 2007.

Fried, Caren-Loebel. *A Perfect Day for an Albatross*. Cornell Lab Publishing Group, 2017.

Frost, Helen. *Sweep Up the Sun*. Candlewick, 2015.

George, Jean Craighead. *The Eagles Are Back*. Dial Books, 2013.

Gianferrari, Maria. *Hawk Rising*. Roaring Brook Press, 2018.

Gibbons, Gail. *Owls*. Holiday House, 2006.

Graham, Bob. *How to Heal a Broken Wing*. Candlewick, 2017.

Gray, Rita. *Have You Heard the Nesting Bird?* HMH Books for Young Readers, 2017.

Gray, Steve. *The Ravenous Raven*. Grand Canyon Association, 2015.

Grolleau, Fabien. *Audubon: On the Wings of the World*. Nobrow Press, 2017.

Henkes, Kevin. *Birds*. Greenwillow Books, 2009.

———. *Egg*. Greenwillow Books, 2017.

Hestermen, Katie. *A Round of Robins*. Nancy Paulsen Books, 2018.

Hiaasen, Carl. *Hoot*. Yearling, 2005.

Hoose, Phillip. *Moonbird*. Farrar, Straus and Giroux, 2012.

———. *The Race to Save the Lord God Bird*. Square Fish, 2016.

Idle, Molly. *Flora and the Flamingo*. Chronicle Books, 2013.

———. *Flora and the Peacocks*. Chronicle Books, 2016.

———. *Flora and the Penguin*. Chronicle Books, 2014.

Jenkins, Martin. *Bird Builds a Nest*. Candlewick, 2018.

Jenkins, Steve. *Animals in Flight*. HMH Books for Young Readers, 2005.

Judge, Lita. *Bird Talk: What Birds Are Saying and Why*. Flash Point, 2012.

———. *Flight School.* Atheneum Books for Young Readers, 2014.

Larson, Jeannette. *Hummingbirds: Fact and Folklore.* Charlesbridge, 2011.

Lewis, Gill. *Wild Wings.* Atheneum Books for Young Readers, 2012.

Lowry, Lois. *Crow Call.* Scholastic Press, 2009.

Lurie, Susan. *Swim, Duck, Swim.* Feiwel & Friends, 2016.

Markle, Sandra. *A Mother's Journey.* Charlesbridge, 2006.

———. *The Long, Long Journey: The Godwit's Amazing Migration.* Millbrook, 2013.

McDermott, Gerald. *Raven: A Trickster Tale from the Pacific Northwest.* HMH Books for Young Readers, 2001.

Pla, Sally. *The Someday Birds.* Harper Collins, 2018.

Prosek, James. *Bird, Butterfly, Eel.* Simon & Schuster Books for Young Readers, 2009.

Rose, Deborah Lee, et, al. *Beauty and the Beak: How Science, Technology, and a 3D-Printed Beak Rescued a Bald Eagle.* Persnickety Press, 2017.

Rosen, Michael. *The Cuckoo's Haiku.* Candlewick, 2009.

Ruddell, Deborah. *Today at the Bluebird Café: A Branchful of Birds.* Margaret K. McElderry Books, 2007.

Sayre, April Pulley. *Vulture View.* Henry Holt and Co., 2007.

———. *Warbler Wave.* Beach Lane Books, 2018.

———. *Woodpecker Wham!* Henry Holt and Co., 2015.

Scanlon, Liz Garton. *One Dark Bird.* Beach Lane Books, 2019.

Schulman, Janet. *Pale Male: Citizen Hawk of New York City.* Knopf, 2008.

Sidman, Joyce. *Red Sings from Treetops.* HMH Books for Young Readers, 2009.

Sill, Cathryn. *About Birds: A Guide for Children.* Peachtree Publishers, 2013.

Singer, Marilyn. *The Company of Crows.* Clarion Books, 2002.

Sonenshine, Randi Miller. *This is the Nest that Wren Built.* Candlewick, 2020.

Stemple, Heidi E.Y. *Counting Birds: The Idea That Helped Save Our Feathered Friends.* Seagrass Press, 2018.

Stewart, Melissa. *A Place for Birds.* Peachtree Publishers, 2015.

———. *Feathers Not Just for Flying.* Charlesbridge, 2014.

Tavares, Matt. *Red and Lulu.* Candlewick, 2017.

Tsong, Jing Jing. *Birds in Hawaii.* Beach House Publishing, 2017.

VanDerwater, Amy Ludwig. *Every Day Birds.* Orchard Books, 2016.

Waddell, Martin. *Owl Babies.* Candlewick, 2002.

Ward, Jennifer. *How to Find a Bird.* Beach Lane, 2020.

———. *Mama Built a Little Nest.* Beach Lane Books, 2014.

Wight, Tamra. *Mystery of the Eagles Nest.* Island Port Press, Inc., 2016.

———. *Mystery on Pine Lake.* Island Port Press, Inc. 2015.

Wolf, Sallie. *The Robin Makes a Laughing Sound: A Birder's Observations.* Charlesbridge, 2010.

Yolen, Jane. *An Egret's Day.* Wordsong, 2010.

———. *On Bird Hill.* Cornell Lab Publishing Group, 2016.

———. *On Duck Pond.* Cornell Lab Publishing Group, 2017.

———. *Owl Moon.* Philomel Books, 1987.

———. *You Nest Here With Me.* Boyds Mills Press, 2015.

WEBSITES

American Birding Association: aba.org

American Bird Conservancy: abcbirds.org

American Ornithological Society: americanornithology.org

Audubon—Nectar Sources by Region: audubon.org/con
tent/nectar-sources-region

Bringing Back the Birds: abcbirds.org/program/bringing-
back-the-birds

Cornell Lab of Ornithology: birds.cornell.edu

Environment for the Americas—International Migratory
Bird Day: birdday.org

FLAP Canada: flap.org

Hummingbirds.net (Lanny Chambers): hummingbirds.net

International Bird Rescue: bird-rescue.org

National Aviary: aviary.org

National Audubon Society: audubon.org

National Wildlife Federation: nwf.org

The Nature Conservancy: nature.org

North American Bird Conservation Initiative (NABCI) /
International Bird Conservation: nabci-us.org/interna
tional-bird-conservation

Project Owlnet through the National Aviary: aviary.org/
project-owlnet

Royal Society for the Protection of Birds: rspb.org.uk

Sierra Club: sierraclub.org

Smithsonian Migratory Bird Center: nationalzoo.si.edu/
migratory-birds

United Nations Environment Program: unep.org

United States Natural Resources Conservation Service:
nrcs.usda.gov

Wildlife Rehabilitators Listed by State: wildliferehabinfo
.org

AMERICAN BIRD
ASSOCIATION CODE OF ETHICS
· ·

THE American Birding Association developed and promotes the following code of birding ethics, which may be freely reproduced for distribution with acknowledgment to the ABA for its development and a link to the ABA website: www.aba.org.

1. Promote the welfare of birds and their environment.

1(a) Support the protection of important bird habitat.

1(b) To avoid stressing birds or exposing them to danger, exercise restraint and caution during observation, photography, sound recording, or filming.

Limit the use of recordings and other methods of attracting birds, and never use such methods in heavily birded areas or for attracting any species that is Threatened, Endangered, of Special Concern, or is rare in your local area.

Keep well back from nests and nesting colonies, roosts, display areas, and important feeding sites. In such sensitive areas, if there is a need for extended observation, photography, filming, or recording, try to use a blind or hide, and take advantage of natural cover.

Use artificial light sparingly for filming or photography, especially for close-ups.

1(c) Before advertising the presence of a rare bird, evaluate the potential for disturbance to the bird, its surroundings, and other people in the area, and proceed only if access can be controlled, disturbance minimized, and permission has been obtained from private landowners. The sites of rare nesting birds should be divulged only to the proper conservation authorities.

1(d) Stay on roads, trails, and paths where they exist; otherwise, keep habitat disturbance to a minimum.

2. Respect the law, and the rights of others.

2(a) Do not enter private property without the owner's explicit permission.

2(b) Follow all laws, rules, and regulations governing use of roads and public areas, both at home and abroad.

2(c) Practice common courtesy in contacts with other people. Your exemplary behavior will generate goodwill with birders and non-birders alike.

3. Ensure that feeders, nest structures, and other artificial bird environments are safe.

3(a) Keep dispensers, water, and food clean and free of decay or disease. It is important to feed birds continually during harsh weather.

3(b) Maintain and clean nest structures regularly.

3(c) If you are attracting birds to an area, ensure the birds are not exposed to predation from cats and other domestic animals or dangers posed by artificial hazards.

4. Group birding, whether organized or impromptu, requires special care.

Each individual in the group, in addition to the obligations spelled out in Items #1 and #2, has responsibilities as a Group Member:

4(a) Respect the interests, rights, and skills of fellow birders, as well as people participating in other legitimate outdoor activities. Freely share your knowledge and experience, except where code 1(c) applies. Be especially helpful to beginning birders.

4(b) If you witness unethical birding behavior, assess the situation and intervene if you think it prudent. When interceding, inform the person(s) of the inappropriate action and attempt, within reason, to have it stopped. If the behavior continues, document it and notify appropriate individuals or organizations.

Group Leader Responsibilities [amateur and professional trips and tours]:

4(c) Be an exemplary ethical role model for the group. Teach through word and example.

4(d) Keep groups to a size that limits impact on the environment and does not interfere with others using the same area.

4(e) Ensure everyone in the group knows of and practices this code.

4(f) Learn and inform the group of any special circumstances applicable to the areas being visited (e.g., no audio playback allowed).

4(g) Acknowledge that professional tour companies bear a special responsibility to place the welfare of birds and the benefits of public knowledge ahead of the company's commercial interests. Ideally, leaders should keep track of tour sightings, document unusual occurrences, and submit records to appropriate organizations.

ABOUT THE AUTHOR

· ·

JENNIFER WARD is the author of more than twenty award-winning books for children—most about nature and many which feature birds—in addition to parenting books that help connect children to nature. Her books have been translated into many languages and have been featured on national television and NPR. She lives with her husband and two dogs, nestled among a canopy of old growth oak forest in Southern Illinois, where she writes full time surrounded by birds and birdsong. Learn more about Jennifer and her books at jenniferwardbooks.com.